MW01595218

INTIMATE
CONVERSATIONS

a personal journey from Genesis to Revelation

An Interactive Devotional and Journal

Kandee Mamula, Ph.D.

Dear Esther,

May you experience in you
All His great delight in you
as He questions you with
love and refreshing over you with
singing (Zephaniah 3:17)

With love,
Kandee

Unless otherwise indicated, all Scripture quotations are taken from the HOLY BIBLE, NEW KING JAMES VERSION (NKJV). Copyright © 1979, 1980, 1982 by Thomas Nelson, Inc., Nashville, TN. Used by permission of Thomas Nelson, Inc.

Scripture taken from the HOLY BIBLE, NEW INTERNATIONAL VERSION (NIV). Copyright © 1973, 1978, 1984 by The International Bible Society, East Brunswick, NJ. Used by permission from Zondervan Bible Publishers.

Scripture taken from THE HOLY BIBLE, THE MESSAGE VERSION (MSG). Copyright © 2003, 2006 by Eugene H. Peterson. Used by permission of NavPress Publishing Group, Colorado Springs, CO.

Copyright © 2014 by Kandee Mamula, Ph.D. All rights reserved. No part of this publication may be reproduced, stored in a retrieval system, or transmitted in any form or by any means, electronic, mechanical, photocopying, recording, or otherwise, without prior permission, except for brief quotations embodied in critical reviews and certain other noncommercial uses permitted by copyright law. For permission requests, please contact kandee@kandeemamula.com.

Cover design by Phill Mamula

Interior design by John Mamula

Author Photo: Ken and Jenn Anderson

Printed in the United States of America by Bookmasters

ISBN # 978-1-4951-2559-1

Ordering Information:
www.kandeemamula.com

This special journey with Abba from Genesis to Revelation is dedicated to my soul mate, Tom, the love of my life, who went home to be with the Lord on September 12, 2012. Tom knew how to live in the center of Abba's love, peace and rest. My life has been greatly blessed, and deeply impacted, by Tom's love and faithful commitment to me and our family.

ACKNOWLEDGEMENTS

To our faithful Abba, who—more than anyone else—wants a loving and intimate relationship with each one of us through Jesus Christ, His Son.

My sincere love and appreciation to each of my family members who came alongside me as I developed this devotional. Your love, encouragement, prayer and insights have deeply touched my life as you traveled along this journey with me and made the devotional better: John Mamula, Angela Baxter, Neoma Harding, Jann Carlson, Linda Mamula, Phill Mamula, Danielle Crihfield, Pat Gettings, Nancy Vaughan, and Sue Campbell.

Special acknowledgment and gratitude for the critical contributions made my dear friends, Editor-in-Chief, Alma Kramer, and Linda Smith, my co-author of *Now I Can Call Him Father* and *Abba's Precious Daughter*. Their insights and editing have greatly contributed to this journey into Abba's heart and truth.

My sincere thankfulness to all my Sisters-in-Christ at Folsom Women's Facility who have prayed for me as I have developed this devotional. Their intercession on my behalf has been very encouraging to me along the way.

My heartfelt appreciation to all my friends who proof read parts of this devotional along the way: Barbara Alvarado, Kristen Bertrand, Patty DeShaw, Linda Gordon, Alma Hawkins, Martha Gunderson, Debbie Naramore, Heather Scott, and Nancy Switzer.

SPECIAL ENCOURAGEMENT FROM ME TO YOU

Each week of this devotional will consist of five days of intimate conversations and two days for resting and reflecting. I encourage you not to rush—this is not a race—it's all about developing a deeper intimacy with your Abba, the One who loves you with an unwavering and unending love. If you treat this journey like a race to be won you will rip yourself off of all Abba wants to show you and experience with you.

If having special time with Abba on a daily basis is a new habit for you, I would strongly encourage you to be accountable to someone by meeting with that person regularly by phone, in a small group, or by text/email. Accountability will help you develop this new habit and also give you an opportunity to share what you experienced with Abba.

Please, please, please—take it slow. I strongly encourage you to ruthlessly and intentionally eliminate hurry in your life as you take this yearlong journey.

CULTIVATING INTIMACY WITH ABBA

Each day will begin with the Word of God to spark your intimate conversation. The following is a process that helps me as I spend quality time with Abba. This process will provide a framework for you to use in the beginning. As time goes on, He will guide you to your own personal process. Enjoy!

Preparation:
- Take only your Bible, pen, and journal and go to a comfortable and quiet place to take some time away from the hustle and bustle of your life.
- Take a few moments to slowly breathe in and out.
- You may want to listen to soothing, instrumental music as you close your eyes and allow your body to relax.

Read:
- Slowly read the daily verse, or short passage, and listen for the word, phrase, or feeling that Abba is showing you to begin your conversation. You may also want to read it in your personal Bible.
- What is catching your attention? What are you experiencing?
- Resist the urge to hurry, judge, or analyze.
- Ponder this word/phrase/feeling and linger there (If other things are coming to your mind, like the things on your daily "to do" list, jot them down in your journal for attention later).

Reflect:
- Ask yourself, "How is this word/phrase touching my mind and heart?" "What is going on in my life right now that needs to hear this word/ phrase?"
- Allow several minutes to pass in silence while you explore your thoughts, feelings, perceptions, and impressions.
- If the passage is a story, you may want to ask yourself, "How do the dynamics of the story connect with my life?"

Respond:
- What is your response to Abba based on what you read, received, and experienced?
- Read the verse/passage one more time, listening for your truest and deepest responses (not the ones you think you should have).
- After a bit of silence, pour out your heart to God in complete honesty— examples: your thankfulness, your joy, your doubts and fears, your frustrations, your anger, your grief, your love for Him, rejoicing, etc.
- You may want to journal at this point.

Rest:

- You can now move into a time of waiting and resting in God's presence, like a baby in his/her parent's secure and comforting embrace. This is a posture of total rest, gratefulness, and abiding in Abba's love and faithfulness.

Resolve:

- As you emerge from this personal encounter with Abba to live life with others, resolve to allow the Holy Spirit to give you deeper understandings throughout the day until it begins to live in you and through you.
- You may want to share the essence of this intimate conversation with another person, or carry a reminder around with you for a period of time that supports your intent to live this out (example: I have a charm on a necklace with the words "Be still and know that I am God." This reminds me to intentionally take time to be still and quiet in order to sense Him as I go about my daily activities).

On the bottom of each journal page are the words: *Read - Reflect - Respond - Rest - Resolve* to help guide you through this process.

This is adapted from a process called Lectio Divina (Sacred Reading).

A PERSONAL NOTE FROM ME TO YOU ...

Dear One,

I don't know about you, but I get busy and it doesn't take much to fill up my day without giving room for special time with Abba. I know He wants these special times with me because the Bible tells me that I was created for the express purpose of knowing Him, experiencing His love, loving Him in return, and representing Him well to others.

I've found that intimacy takes time together through sharing everything about life: hopes, dreams, ambitions, failures, joys, and sorrows. Many days I really do want to share personal time with Abba—but then the day gets full of other things. By the end of the day I'm so tired I just fall into bed and say a quick, "Thank you, Lord" and quickly nod off to sleep. It seems like when I don't make time for Him, it's just a big rip off for both of us.

I experienced a life-changing moment on September 12, 2012. You probably have had one or two in your life. A moment that stopped you in your tracks, and caused you to either run from God, or run desperately into His arms, never wanting to leave. This life-changer for me was the day my soul mate, Tom, went home to be with the Lord. On that day in September my life, as I knew it, changed forever. This devotional book comes out of my first year without Tom and the deepening of my relationship with Abba along the way.

My heart's desire in developing this devotional is to encourage you along your life's journey to set aside time on a daily basis to have intimate conversations with your Creator, Abba, in the context of rest, solitude and stillness. These special times will greatly enrich your life and the many lives that you touch.

A fellow sojourner,

Kandee

A PERSONAL MESSAGE FROM ABBA ...

Dear Precious Son/Daughter,

You are so very precious to Me. I want you to know that I'm really looking forward to our daily intimate conversations as we journey together through My love letter to you—the Holy Bible. I invite you to saturate yourself in the revelation of My love, forgiveness and grace.

My number one desire is to cultivate a heart-to-heart relationship with you. I want you to know that during our special quiet times together I want to dispel any misconceptions you have about Me, and of yourself, that hinders closeness in our relationship.

Please keep in mind that I have made you very unique. I have given you your own very special set of fingerprints as a sign from Me that you are one-of-a-kind. Knowing that, please realize that our intimate conversations are not limited to our quiet times together. In fact, you have been "wired" by Me to sense Me throughout the day in various ways such as sensing impressions or feelings, seeing a picture in your mind, hearing an audible word or phrase, or experiencing Me through my creation (hearing a bird sing, smelling the aroma of a flower, hearing children's laughter, etc.).

Please know that I am looking forward to our special times together.

I love you and believe in you!

Abba

THE IMPORTANCE OF DAILY TIME WITH ABBA

Fathers play an invaluable and irreplaceable role in the development of their children. One of the critical components in the development of spiritual and emotional maturity is time spent with Abba, loving, nurturing, providing, disciplining, protecting, and guiding you through His Word.

I have used the term "Abba" in this devotional because its biblical meaning in Aramaic and Greek expresses the special relationship that exists between a believer and God the Father. It is a term of intimacy and is translated 'daddy' in English.

This devotional's goal is to provide daily opportunities for you, Abba's precious child, to spend time with your Heavenly Father, in order to develop a close and trusting relationship with Him. The development of intimacy between you and Abba will profoundly affect every aspect of your life.

ENJOY each intimate conversation with your Heavenly Father and be transformed in the process!

GENESIS: THEME-BEGINNINGS

Genesis means "beginning." Written by Moses to the people of Israel, this book tells the story of the beginning of the world, the beginning of sin, and the beginning of God's plan for redeeming sinful people.

Genesis reveals that God longs to have an intimate relationship with us. His divine presence and promises point us toward hope in spite of our sins, failures, and struggles.

Day #1: _____ **(date)**

Let's begin our intimate conversation today with ...

Genesis 1:1, "In the beginning God created the heavens and the earth."

I love you!

Abba

_____

_____

_____

_____

_____

_____

_____

_____

_____

_____

_____

_____

_____

_____

_____

_____

_____

_____

_____

_____

Day #2: _____ **(date)**

Let's begin our intimate conversation today with ...

Genesis 1:27-28, "So God created man in His own image; in the image of God He created him; male and female He created them. Then God blessed them, and God said to them, 'Be fruitful and multiply; fill the earth and subdue it; have dominion over the fish of the sea, over the birds of the air, and over every living thing that moves on the earth.'"

I love you!

Abba

_____

_____

_____

_____

_____

_____

_____

_____

_____

_____

_____

_____

_____

_____

_____

_____

_____

_____

_____

_____

_____

_____

Day #3: _____ **(date)**

Let's begin our intimate conversation today with …

Genesis 3:2-7 (NIV), "The woman said to the serpent, 'We may eat fruit from the trees in the garden, but God did say, 'You must not eat fruit from the tree that is in the middle of the garden, and you must not touch it, or you will die." 'You will not surely die,' the serpent said to the woman. 'For God knows that when you eat of it your eyes will be opened, and you will be like God, knowing good and evil.' When the woman saw that the fruit of the tree was good for food and pleasing to the eye, and also desirable for gaining wisdom, she took some and ate it. She also gave some to her husband, who was with her, and he ate it. Then the eyes of both of them were opened, and they realized they were naked; so they sewed fig leaves together and made coverings for themselves."

I love you!

Abba

_____

_____

_____

_____

_____

_____

_____

_____

_____

_____

_____

_____

_____

_____

_____

_____

_____

_____

_____

_____

Day #4: _____ (date)

Let's begin our intimate conversation today with ...

Genesis 22:9-14 (NIV), "When they (Abraham and Isaac) reached the place God had told him about, Abraham built an altar there and arranged the wood on it. He bound his son Isaac and laid him on the altar, on top of the wood. Then he reached out his hand and took the knife to slay his son. But the angel of the LORD called out to him from heaven, 'Abraham! Abraham!' 'Here I am,' he replied. 'Do not lay a hand on the boy,' he said. 'Do not do anything to him. Now I know that you fear God, because you have not withheld from me your son, your only son.' Abraham looked up and there in a thicket he saw a ram caught by its horns. He went over and took the ram and sacrificed it as a burnt offering instead of his son. So Abraham called that place The LORD Will Provide. ..."

I love you!

Abba

_____

_____

_____

_____

_____

_____

_____

_____

_____

_____

_____

_____

_____

_____

_____

_____

_____

_____

_____

_____

Day #5: _____ **(date)**

Let's begin our intimate conversation today with ...

Genesis 50:20 (NIV), (Joseph speaking): "You intended to harm me, but God intended it for good to accomplish what is now being done, the saving of many lives."

I love you!

Abba

_____

_____

_____

_____

_____

_____

_____

_____

_____

_____

_____

_____

_____

_____

_____

_____

_____

_____

_____

_____

_____

_____

_____

Days #6 & #7: Rest & Reflect _____(dates)

Take some time to review what we shared over the past five days and record any new thoughts, feelings, insights, impressions, and responses. How did these intimate conversations impact you? How did they impact others as you interacted with them? What are you most grateful for?

I love you!

Abba

_____

_____

_____

_____

_____

_____

_____

_____

_____

_____

_____

_____

_____

_____

_____

_____

_____

_____

_____

_____

_____

_____

_____

_____

EXODUS: THEME— DELIVERANCE

Exodus means "the way out" and paints a vivid picture of the journey from God's deliverance of His people out of slavery to the beginning of their 40-year trek to the Promised Land.

Throughout this special journey God intervenes again and again with grace and deliverance---reminding us that no one is hopelessly beyond the reach of His loving touch. He alone can set people free.

Day #8: _____ **(date)**

Let's begin our intimate conversation today with ...

Exodus 3:7-8, "And the LORD said: 'I have surely seen the oppression of My people who are in Egypt, and have heard their cry because of their taskmasters, for I know their sorrows. So I have come down to deliver them out of the hand of the Egyptians, and to bring them up from that land to a good and large land, to a land flowing with milk and honey...'"

I love you!

Abba

_____

_____

_____

_____

_____

_____

_____

_____

_____

_____

_____

_____

_____

_____

_____

_____

Day #9: _____ **(date)**

Let's begin our intimate conversation today with ...

Exodus 12:1, 12-13 (MSG), "God said to Moses and Aaron while still in Egypt ...
'I will go through the land of Egypt on this night and strike down every firstborn
in the land of Egypt, whether human or animal, and bring judgment on all the
gods of Egypt. I am GOD. The blood will serve as a sign on the houses where you
live. When I see the blood I will pass over you— no disaster will touch you when
I strike the land of Egypt.'"

I love you!

Abba

_____

_____

_____

_____

_____

_____

_____

_____

_____

_____

_____

_____

_____

_____

_____

_____

_____

_____

_____

_____

_____

Day #10: _____ **(date)**

Let's begin our intimate conversation today with ...

Exodus 14:21-22, "Then Moses stretched out his hand over the sea; and the LORD caused the sea to go back by a strong east wind all that night, and made the sea into dry land, and the waters were divided. So the children of Israel went into the midst of the sea on the dry ground, and the waters were a wall to them on their right hand and on their left."

I love you!

Abba

_____

_____

_____

_____

_____

_____

_____

_____

_____

_____

_____

_____

_____

_____

_____

_____

_____

_____

_____

_____

_____

_____

Day #11: _____ **(date)**

Let's begin our intimate conversation today with ...

Exodus 20:1-3 (NIV), "And God spoke all these words: 'I am the LORD your God, who brought you out of Egypt, out of the land of slavery. You shall have no other gods before me.'"

I love you!

Abba

_____

_____

_____

_____

_____

_____

_____

_____

_____

_____

_____

_____

_____

_____

_____

_____

_____

_____

_____

_____

_____

_____

_____

_____

Day #12: _____(date)

Let's begin our intimate conversation today with ...

Exodus 40:38, "For the cloud of the LORD was above the tabernacle by day, and fire was over it by night, in the sight of all the house of Israel, throughout all their journeys."

I love you!

Abba

_____

_____

_____

_____

_____

_____

_____

_____

_____

_____

_____

_____

_____

_____

_____

_____

_____

_____

_____

_____

_____

_____

_____

Days #13 & #14: Rest & Reflect _____(dates)

Take some time to review what we shared over the past five days and record
any new thoughts, feelings, insights, impressions, and responses. How did
these intimate conversations impact you? How did they impact others as you
interacted with them? What are you most grateful for?

I love you!

Abba

_____

_____

_____

_____

_____

_____

_____

_____

_____

_____

_____

_____

_____

_____

_____

_____

_____

_____

_____

_____

_____

_____

_____

_____

_____

LEVITICUS: THEME— HOLINESS

This book calls God's people to holiness because He is holy. It is permeated with the sanctity of God, the holiness of His character, and the definite necessity of His people to approach Him in purity of heart and mind. God's great desire for fellowship with His people is clearly seen in the specific instructions regarding the sacrificial system prior to the sacrifice of Jesus Christ on the cross in the New Testament.

This book's instructions show that every aspect of our lives---moral, physical, and spiritual---is important to God.

Day #15: _____ **(date)**

Let's begin our intimate conversation today with ...

Leviticus 17:11 (NIV), "For the life of a creature is in the blood, and I have given it to you to make atonement for yourselves on the altar; it is the blood that makes atonement for one's life."

I love you!

Abba

_____

_____

_____

_____

_____

_____

_____

_____

_____

_____

_____

_____

_____

_____

_____

Day #16: _____ **(date)**

Let's begin our intimate conversation today with ...

Leviticus 19:1 (NIV), "The LORD said to Moses, 'Speak to the entire assembly of Israel and say to them: 'Be holy because I, the LORD your God, am holy.'"

I love you!

Abba

_____

_____

_____

_____

_____

_____

_____

_____

_____

_____

_____

_____

_____

_____

_____

_____

_____

_____

_____

_____

_____

_____

_____

_____

_____

NUMBERS: THEME- GOD'S GUIDING PRESENCE

This book shows God's faithfulness and protection for the Israelites, even though they exhibited fear on their journey to the Promised Land. Their fears led them to unbelief and rebellion. God's perfect judgment caused them to wander in the desert for forty years before entering the Promised Land.

Day #17: _____ **(date)**

Let's begin our intimate conversation today with ...

Numbers 13:1, 27-28; 14:11 (NIV), "The LORD said to Moses, 'Send some men to explore the land of Canaan, which I am giving to the Israelites. From each ancestral tribe send one of its leaders.' ...They gave Moses this account: 'We went into the land to which you sent us, and it does flow with milk and honey! Here is its fruit. But the people who live there are powerful, and the cities are fortified and very large. We even saw descendants of Anak there.' ... The LORD said to Moses, 'How long will these people treat me with contempt? How long will they refuse to believe in me, in spite of all the miraculous signs I have performed among them?'"

I love you!

Abba

_____

_____

_____

_____

_____

_____

_____

_____

_____

_____

_____

_____

_____

_____

Day #18: _____(date)

Let's begin our intimate conversation today with ...

Caleb & Joshua speak out in faith: Numbers 14:6- 9 (NIV), "Joshua son of Nun and Caleb son of Jephunneh, who were among those who had explored the land, tore their clothes and said to the entire Israelite assembly, 'The land we passed through and explored is exceedingly good. If the LORD is pleased with us, he will lead us into that land, a land flowing with milk and honey, and will give it to us. Only do not rebel against the LORD. And do not be afraid of the people of the land, because we will swallow them up. Their protection is gone, but the LORD is with us. Do not be afraid of them.'"

I love you!

Abba

_____

_____

_____

_____

_____

_____

_____

_____

_____

_____

_____

_____

_____

_____

_____

_____

_____

_____

_____

_____

_____

Day #19: _____(date)

Let's begin our intimate conversation today with ...

Numbers 23:19 (MSG), "God is not man, one given to lies, and not a son of man changing his mind. Does he speak and not do what he says? Does he promise and not come through?"

I love you!

Abba

_____

_____

_____

_____

_____

_____

_____

_____

_____

_____

_____

_____

_____

_____

_____

_____

_____

_____

_____

_____

_____

_____

_____

Days #20 & #21: Rest and Reflect _____(dates)

Take some time to review what we shared over the past five days and record any new thoughts, feelings, insights, impressions, and responses. How did these intimate conversations impact you? How did they impact others as you interacted with them? What are you most grateful for?

I love you!

Abba

_____

_____

_____

_____

_____

_____

_____

_____

_____

_____

_____

_____

_____

_____

_____

_____

_____

_____

_____

_____

_____

_____

_____

_____

_____

DEUTERONOMY: THEME- OBEDIENCE BRINGS BLESSINGS AND DISOBEDIENCE BRINGS CURSINGS

This book is a strong call to allegiance to God. The older generation of Israelites never reached the Promised Land because of fear and unbelief. The younger generation had the opportunity to learn from their parent's errors and experience God's blessings in their lives.

This book is a great reminder that God will lead us out of the wildernesses of our lives when we trust and obey Him.

Day #22: _____(date)

Let's begin our intimate conversation today with ...

Deuteronomy 2:7 (MSG), "GOD, your God, has blessed you in everything you have done. He has guarded you in your travels through this immense wilderness. For forty years now, GOD, your God, has been right here with you. You haven't lacked one thing."

I love you!

Abba

_____

_____

_____

_____

_____

_____

_____

_____

_____

_____

_____

_____

_____

_____

_____

Day #23: _____ (date)

Let's begin our intimate conversation today with ...

Deuteronomy 5:7, "You shall have no other gods before Me."

I love you!

Abba

_____

_____

_____

_____

_____

_____

_____

_____

_____

_____

_____

_____

_____

_____

_____

_____

_____

_____

_____

_____

_____

_____

_____

_____

_____

Day #24: _____ **(date)**

Let's begin our intimate conversation today with ...

Deuteronomy 10:12-13 (MSG), "So now Israel, what do you think GOD expects from you? Just this: Live in his presence in holy reverence, follow the road he sets out for you, love him, serve GOD, your God, with everything you have in you, obey the commandments and regulations of GOD that I'm commanding you today—live a good life."

I love you!

Abba

_____

_____

_____

_____

_____

_____

_____

_____

_____

_____

_____

_____

_____

_____

_____

_____

_____

_____

_____

_____

_____

_____

Day #25: _____ **(date)**

Let's begin our intimate conversation today with ...

Deuteronomy 30:19-20 (NIV), "This day I call heaven and earth as witnesses against you that I have set before you life and death, blessings and curses. Now choose life, so that you and your children may live and that you may love the LORD your God, listen to his voice, and hold fast to him. For the LORD is your life, and he will give you many years in the land he swore to give to your fathers, Abraham, Isaac, and Jacob."

I love you!

Abba

_____

_____

_____

_____

_____

_____

_____

_____

_____

_____

_____

_____

_____

_____

_____

_____

_____

_____

_____

_____

_____

Day #26: _____ (date)

Let's begin our intimate conversation today with ...

Deuteronomy 31:6 (MSG), "Be strong. Take courage. Don't be intimidated. Don't give them a second thought because GOD, your God, is striding ahead of you. He's right there with you. He won't let you down; he won't leave you."

I love you!

Abba

_____

_____

_____

_____

_____

_____

_____

_____

_____

_____

_____

_____

_____

_____

_____

_____

_____

_____

_____

_____

_____

_____

_____

_____

_____

Days #27 & #28: Rest and Reflect _____(dates)

Take some time to review what we shared over the past five days and record any new thoughts, feelings, insights, impressions, and responses. How did these intimate conversations impact you? How did they impact others as you interacted with them? What are you most grateful for?

I love you!

Abba

_____

_____

_____

_____

_____

_____

_____

_____

_____

_____

_____

_____

_____

_____

_____

_____

_____

_____

_____

_____

_____

_____

_____

Day #29: _____ **(date)**

Let's begin our intimate conversation today with ...

Deuteronomy 32:3-4, "For I proclaim the name of the LORD: Ascribe greatness to our God. He is the Rock. His work is perfect; For all His ways are justice, A God of truth and without injustice; Righteous and upright is He."

I love you!

Abba

_____

_____

_____

_____

_____

_____

_____

_____

_____

_____

_____

_____

_____

_____

_____

_____

_____

_____

_____

_____

_____

_____

JOSHUA: THEME- CONQUEST

Joshua chronicles the period from Israel's entrance into Canaan through the conquest, division, and settlement of the Promised Land. As the Israelites obeyed God, the blessings of victory, inheritance, abundant provision, peace and rest all came to them.

The book of Joshua teaches us not to be content with a timid faith. Throughout our lives God will ask us to believe for the incredible and do the impossible by putting our wholehearted faith in Him.

Day #30: _____ (date)

Let's begin our intimate conversation today with ...

Joshua 1:10-11 (NIV), "So Joshua ordered the officers of the people: 'Go through the camp and tell the people, 'Get your provisions ready. Three days from now you will cross the Jordan here to go in and take possession of the land the LORD your God is giving you for your own.'"

I love you!

Abba

_____

_____

_____

_____

_____

_____

_____

_____

_____

_____

_____

_____

_____

_____

_____

Day #31: _____ (date)

Let's begin our intimate conversation today with ...

Joshua 24:14-15, "Now therefore, fear the LORD, serve Him in sincerity and in truth, and put away the gods which your fathers served on the other side of the River and in Egypt. Serve the LORD! And if it seems evil to you to serve the LORD, choose for yourselves this day whom you will serve, whether the gods which your fathers served that were on the other side of the River, or the gods of the Amorites, in whose land you dwell. But as for me and my house, we will serve the LORD."

I love you!

Abba

_____

_____

_____

_____

_____

_____

_____

_____

_____

_____

_____

_____

_____

_____

_____

_____

_____

_____

_____

_____

_____

_____

JUDGES: THEMES- APOSTASY, OPPRESSION, REPENTANCE AND DELIVERANCE

The Book of Judges covers a chaotic period in Israel's history. After conquering and settling the Promised Land, the Israelites let down their guard. They gave in to cultural pressures and began serving pagan gods. The Israelites repeatedly rebelled against God and set in motion a recurring cycle of events: apostasy, oppression, repentance, and deliverance.

This book graphically portrays the character of the Lord in His dealings with His people. In righteousness, the Lord punished them for their sin. But in His love and mercy, He delivered them in response to their penitent cry.

Day #32: _____ (date)

Let's begin our intimate conversation today with ...

Judges 2:1-4, "Then the Angel of the LORD came up from Gilgal and Bochim, and said: 'I led you up from Egypt and brought you to the land of which I swore to your fathers; and I said, 'I will never break My covenant with you. And you shall make no covenant with the inhabitants of this land; you shall tear down their altars.' But you have not obeyed my voice. Why have you done this? Therefore I also said, 'I will not drive them out before you; but they shall be thorns in your side, and their gods shall be a snare to you.' So it was, when the Angel of the LORD spoke these words to all the children of Israel, that the people lifted up their voices and wept."

I love you!

Abba

_____

_____

_____

_____

_____

_____

_____

_____

_____

Day #33: _____ (date)

Let's begin our intimate conversation today with ...

Judges 3:7-9, "So the children of Israel did evil in the sight of the LORD. They forgot the LORD their God, and served the Baals and Asherahs. ... When the children of Israel cried out to the LORD, the LORD raised up a deliverer for the children of Israel, who delivered them: Othniel the son of Kenaz, Caleb's younger brother."

I love you!

Abba

_____

_____

_____

_____

_____

_____

_____

_____

_____

_____

_____

_____

_____

_____

_____

_____

_____

_____

_____

_____

_____

_____

Days #34 & #35: Rest and Reflect _____(dates)

Take some time to review what we shared over the past five days and record any new thoughts, feelings, insights, impressions, and responses. How did these intimate conversations impact you? How did they impact others as you interacted with them? What are you most grateful for?

I love you!

Abba

_____

_____

_____

_____

_____

_____

_____

_____

_____

_____

_____

_____

_____

_____

_____

_____

_____

_____

_____

_____

_____

_____

Day #36: _____ **(date)**

Let's begin our intimate conversation today with ...

Judges 21:25 (MSG), "At that time there was no king in Israel. People did whatever they felt like doing."

I love you!

Abba

RUTH: THEME- GOD'S SOVEREIGN INTERVENTION BRINGS UNIVERSAL REDEMPTION

This book was written during the time of the judges. Its main focus is the sovereignty of God, with an emphasis on God's sustaining mercy. It gives an account of love and loyalty and how God uses ordinary people to accomplish extraordinary things. It begins with famine, death, and loss but it ends with Boaz, the "kinsman-redeemer", bringing about Ruth's restoration.

Day #37: _____ **(date)**

Let's begin our intimate conversation today with ...

Ruth 1:16-17 (NIV), "But Ruth replied (to Naomi), 'Don't urge me to leave you or to turn back from you. Where you go I will go, and where you stay I will stay. Your people will be my people and your God my God. Where you die I will die, and there I will be buried. May the LORD deal with me, be it ever so severely, if anything but death separates you and me.'"

I love you!

Abba

_____

_____

_____

_____

_____

_____

_____

_____

_____

_____

_____

_____

_____

_____

_____

_____

_____

Day #38: _____ (date)

Let's begin our intimate conversation today with ...

Ruth 2:11-12 (NIV), "Boaz replied, 'I've been told all about what you have done for your mother-in-law since the death of your husband—how you left your father and mother and your homeland and came to live with a people you did not know before. May the LORD repay you for what you have done. May you be richly rewarded by the LORD, the God of Israel, under whose wings you have come to take refuge.'"

I love you!

Abba

_____

_____

_____

_____

_____

_____

_____

_____

_____

_____

_____

_____

_____

_____

_____

_____

_____

_____

_____

_____

_____

Day #39: _____ (date)

Let's begin our intimate conversation today with ...

Ruth 4:9-10, 13-14 (NIV), "Then Boaz announced to the elders and all the people, 'Today you are witnesses that I have bought from Naomi all the property of Elimelech, Kilion and Mahlon. I have also acquired Ruth the Moabitess, Mahlon's widow, as my wife, in order to maintain the name of the dead with his property, so that his name will not disappear from among his family or from the town records. Today you are witnesses!' ... So Boaz took Ruth and she became his wife. Then he went to her, and the LORD enabled her to conceive, and she gave birth to a son. The women said to Naomi: 'Praise be to the LORD, who this day has not left you without a kinsman-redeemer. May he become famous throughout Israel!'"

I love you!

Abba

_____

_____

_____

_____

_____

_____

_____

_____

_____

_____

_____

_____

_____

_____

_____

_____

_____

_____

_____

1 SAMUEL: THEME- GOD IS WORKING IN HISTORY

This book describes a time when the Israelites get discouraged with having judges and cry out to have a king. God instructs the prophet Samuel to anoint Saul as their first king. His reign begins well, but he soon begins living a disobedient lifestyle. While this is happening God is preparing a new king for Israel---a young shepherd boy named David. David grows in faithfulness while Saul sinks into more and more depravity.

The lives of Saul and David are prime examples that show us we each have opportunities to make a mess or make a difference.

Day #40: _____ (date)

Let's begin our intimate conversation today with ...

1 Samuel 15:22-24 (MSG), "Then Samuel said, 'Do you think all GOD wants are sacrifices—empty rituals just for show? He wants you to listen to him! Plain listening is the thing, not staging a lavish religious production. Not doing what GOD tells you is far worse than fooling around in the occult. Getting self-important around GOD is far worse than making deals with your dead ancestors. Because you said No to GOD's command, he says No to your kingship.' Saul gave in and confessed, 'I've sinned. I've trampled roughshod over GOD's Word and your instructions. I cared more about pleasing the people. I let them tell me what to do.'"

I love you!

Abba

_____

_____

_____

_____

_____

_____

_____

_____

_____

Days #41 & #42: Rest and Reflect _____(dates)

Take some time to review what we shared over the past five days and record any new thoughts, feelings, insights, impressions, and responses. How did these intimate conversations impact you? How did they impact others as you interacted with them? What are you most grateful for?

I love you!

Abba

_____

_____

_____

_____

_____

_____

_____

_____

_____

_____

_____

_____

_____

_____

_____

_____

_____

_____

_____

_____

_____

Day #43: _____ **(date)**

Let's begin our intimate conversation today with ...

1 Samuel 16:7 (NIV), "But the LORD said to Samuel, '... The LORD does not look at the things man looks at. Man looks at the outward appearance, but the LORD looks at the heart.'"

I love you!

Abba

_____

_____

_____

_____

_____

_____

_____

_____

_____

_____

_____

_____

_____

_____

_____

_____

_____

_____

_____

_____

_____

_____

_____

_____

_____

Day #44: _____ (date)

Let's begin our intimate conversation today with ...

1 Samuel 17:48-49, 51 (NIV), "As the Philistine (Goliath) moved closer to attack him, David ran quickly toward the battle line to meet him. Reaching into his bag and taking out a stone, he slung it and struck the Philistine on the forehead. The stone sank into his forehead, and he fell facedown on the ground. ...David ran and stood over him. He took hold of the Philistine's sword and drew it from the scabbard. After he killed him, he cut off his head with the sword. When the Philistines saw that their hero was dead, they turned and ran."

I love you!

Abba

_____

_____

_____

_____

_____

_____

_____

_____

_____

_____

_____

_____

_____

_____

_____

_____

_____

_____

_____

_____

2 SAMUEL: THEME— UNIFICATION

2 Samuel presents the story of King David's 40-year reign. It shows David both as a model king and an imperfect person who makes sinful choices; a life that was driven by both holy and impure passions. A critical emphasis in this book is the fact that although human beings are sinful, and suffer the consequences, God still works through them to accomplish His redemptive purposes.

Day #45: _____ **(date)**

Let's begin our intimate conversation today with ...

2 Samuel 6:12, 14-15 (NIV), "Now King David was told, 'The LORD has blessed the house of Obed-Edom and everything he has, because of the ark of God.' So David went down and brought up the ark of God from the house of Obed-Edom to the City of David with rejoicing. ...David, wearing a linen ephod, danced before the LORD with all his might, while he and the entire house of Israel brought up the ark of the LORD with shouts and the sound of trumpets."

I love you!

Abba

_____

_____

_____

_____

_____

_____

_____

_____

_____

_____

_____

_____

_____

Day #46: _____ (date)

Let's begin our intimate conversation today with ...

2 Samuel 22:2-4, "And he (David) said: 'The LORD is my rock and my fortress and my deliverer; The God of my strength, in whom I will trust; My shield and the horn of my salvation, My stronghold and my refuge; My Savior, You save me from violence. I will call upon the LORD, who is worthy to be praised; So shall I be saved from my enemies.'"

I love you!

Abba

_____

_____

_____

_____

_____

_____

_____

_____

_____

_____

_____

_____

_____

_____

_____

_____

_____

_____

_____

_____

Day #47: _____ (date)

Let's begin our intimate conversation today with ...

2 Samuel 22:31 (NIV), "As for God, his way is perfect; the word of the LORD is flawless. He is a shield for all who take refuge in him."

I love you!

Abba

_____

_____

_____

_____

_____

_____

_____

_____

_____

_____

_____

_____

_____

_____

_____

_____

_____

_____

_____

_____

_____

_____

_____

_____

_____

Days #48 and #49: Rest and Reflect _____(dates)

Take some time to review what we shared over the past five days and record any new thoughts, feelings, insights, impressions, and responses. How did these intimate conversations impact you? How did they impact others as you interacted with them? What are you most grateful for?

I love you!

Abba

_____

_____

_____

_____

_____

_____

_____

_____

_____

_____

_____

_____

_____

_____

_____

_____

_____

_____

_____

_____

_____

I KINGS: THEME- DISRUPTION

First Kings records the turbulent experiences of God's people for about one hundred and twenty years after the death of King David. During this difficult time there was great change and upheaval. There were internal struggles, as well as external pressures. The result was the once stable kingdom became split in two: Judah and Israel. This book shows the critical importance of obedience to God and the painful consequences of disobedience.

Day #50: _____ **(date)**

Let's begin our intimate conversation today with ...

1 Kings 2:1-3 (NIV), "When the time drew near for David to die, he gave a charge to Solomon his son. 'I am about to go the way of all the earth,' he said. 'So be strong, show yourself a man, and observe what the LORD your God requires: Walk in his ways, and keep his decrees and commands, his laws and requirements, as written in the Law of Moses, so that you may prosper in all you do and wherever you go.'"

I love you!

Abba

_____

_____

_____

_____

_____

_____

_____

_____

_____

_____

_____

_____

_____

_____

Day #51: _____ (date)

Let's begin our intimate conversation today with ...

1 Kings 3:7-9 (MSG), "'And now here I (Solomon) am: GOD, my God, you have made me, your servant, ruler of the kingdom in place of David my father. I'm too young for this, a mere child! I don't know the ropes, hardly know the 'ins' and 'outs' of this job. And here I am, set down in the middle of the people you've chosen, a great people—far too many to ever count. Here's what I want: Give me a God-listening heart so I can lead your people well, discerning the difference between good and evil. For who on their own is capable of leading your glorious people?'"

I love you!

Abba

_____

_____

_____

_____

_____

_____

_____

_____

_____

_____

_____

_____

_____

_____

_____

_____

_____

_____

_____

Day #52: _____ (date)

Let's begin our intimate conversation today with …

I Kings 9:3 (MSG), "And GOD said to him (Solomon), 'I've listened to and received all your prayers, your ever-so-passionate prayers. I've sanctified this Temple that you have built: My Name is stamped on it forever; my eyes are on it and my heart in it always.'"

I love you!

Abba

_____

_____

_____

_____

_____

_____

_____

_____

_____

_____

_____

_____

_____

_____

_____

_____

_____

_____

_____

_____

_____

_____

_____

_____

_____

2 KINGS: THEME- DISPERSION

This book shows the final overthrow and deportation of God's people: Israel to Assyria and Judah to Babylon. This captivity to foreign pagan nations was the inevitable consequence of God's people consistently violating God's covenant, especially through idolatry and pagan worship. Against this backdrop of godless living, the mercy of God is clearly seen.

Day #53: _____ **(date)**

Let's begin our intimate conversation today with ...

2 Kings 17:7-8 (MSG), "The exile came about because of sin: The children of Israel sinned against GOD, their God, who had delivered them from Egypt and the brutal oppression of Pharaoh king of Egypt. They took up with other gods, fell in with the ways of life of the pagan nations GOD had chased off, and went along with whatever their kings did."

I love you!

Abba

_____

_____

_____

_____

_____

_____

_____

_____

_____

_____

_____

_____

_____

_____

_____

_____

Day #54: _____ (date)

Let's begin our intimate conversation today with ...

2 Kings 23:25 (MSG), "There was no king to compare with Josiah—neither before nor after—a king who turned in total repentant obedience to GOD, heart and mind and strength, following the instructions revealed to and written by Moses. The world would never again see a king like Josiah."

I love you!

Abba

_____

_____

_____

_____

_____

_____

_____

_____

_____

_____

_____

_____

_____

_____

_____

_____

_____

_____

_____

_____

_____

_____

_____

Days #55 & #56: Rest and Reflect _____(dates)

Take some time to review what we shared over the past five days and record any new thoughts, feelings, insights, impressions, and responses. How did these intimate conversations impact you? How did they impact others as you interacted with them? What are you most grateful for?

I love you!

Abba

_____

_____

_____

_____

_____

_____

_____

_____

_____

_____

_____

_____

_____

_____

_____

_____

_____

_____

_____

_____

_____

_____

1 CHRONICLES: THEME- ENCOURAGEMENT & EXHORTATION FROM JUDAH'S SPIRITUAL HISTORY

This book contains a compilation of genealogies from Adam to the crowning of David's son, Solomon, as king. In order to encourage and give hope to those coming back from exile, it reveals how God has always been faithful to His people. It encourages us to trust Him, and all His promises, especially when we feel defeated, discouraged, and weary. It also exhorts us to learn from the mistakes of others in the past.

Day #57: _____ **(date)**

Let's begin our intimate conversation today with ...

1 Chronicles 16:23-25a, "Sing to the LORD, all the earth; Proclaim the good news of His salvation from day to day. Declare His glory among the nations, His wonders among all peoples. For the LORD is great and greatly to be praised."

I love you!

Abba

_____

_____

_____

_____

_____

_____

_____

_____

_____

_____

_____

_____

_____

_____

_____

_____

Day #58: _____ (date)

Let's begin our intimate conversation today with ...

1 Chronicles 28:9 (David speaking), "As for you, my son Solomon, know the God of your father, and serve Him with a loyal heart and with a willing mind; for the LORD searches all hearts and understands all the intent of the thoughts. If you seek Him, He will be found by you; but if you forsake Him, He will cast you off forever."

I love you!

Abba

_____

_____

_____

_____

_____

_____

_____

_____

_____

_____

_____

_____

_____

_____

_____

_____

_____

_____

_____

_____

_____

Day #59 _____ (date)

Let's begin our intimate conversation today with ...

1 Chronicles 28:20, "And David said to his son Solomon, 'Be strong and of good courage, and do it; do not fear nor be dismayed, for the LORD God—my God—will be with you. He will not leave you nor forsake you, until you have finished all the work for the service of the house of the LORD.'"

I love you!

Abba

2 CHRONICLES: THEME— ENCOURAGEMENT AND EXHORTATION TO THE RETURNING EXILES

This book is a continuation of I Chronicles, continuing the encouragement and exhortation to those returning from exile to Jerusalem. The building of the temple is a central theme. One unique focus of this book is that God is our sovereign deliverer. It reminds us that circumstances change and people fail, but God's promises are forever.

Day #60: _____ **(date)**

Let's begin our intimate conversation today with …

2 Chronicles 1:7-10 (MSG), "That night God appeared to Solomon. God said, 'What do you want from me? Ask.' Solomon answered, 'You were extravagantly generous with David my father, and now you have made me king in his place. Establish, God, the words you spoke to my father, for you've given me a staggering task, ruling this mob of people. Yes, give me wisdom and knowledge as I come and go among this people—for who on his own is capable of leading these, your glorious people?'"

I love you!

Abba

_____

_____

_____

_____

_____

_____

_____

_____

_____

_____

_____

_____

Day #61: _____ (date)

Let's begin our intimate conversation today with ...

2 Chronicles 1:11-12 (MSG), "God answered Solomon, 'This is what has come out of your heart: You didn't grasp for money, wealth, fame, and the doom of your enemies; you didn't even ask for a long life. You asked for wisdom and knowledge so you could govern well my people over whom I've made you king. Because of this, you get what you asked for—wisdom and knowledge. And I'm presenting you the rest as a bonus—money, wealth, and fame beyond anything the kings before or after you had or will have.'"

I love you!

Abba

_____

_____

_____

_____

_____

_____

_____

_____

_____

_____

_____

_____

_____

_____

_____

_____

_____

_____

_____

_____

Days #62 & #63: Rest & Reflect _____(dates)

Take some time to review what we shared over the past five days and record any new thoughts, feelings, insights, impressions, and responses. How did these intimate conversations impact you? How did they impact others as you interacted with them? What are you most grateful for?

I love you!

Abba

_____

_____

_____

_____

_____

_____

_____

_____

_____

_____

_____

_____

_____

_____

_____

_____

_____

_____

_____

_____

_____

_____

Day #64: _____ (date)

Let's begin our intimate conversation today with ...

2 Chronicles 7:14, "If my people who are called by My name will humble themselves, and pray and seek My face, and turn from their wicked ways, then I will hear from heaven, and will forgive their sin and heal their land."

I love you!

Abba

_____

_____

_____

_____

_____

_____

_____

_____

_____

_____

_____

_____

_____

_____

_____

_____

_____

_____

_____

_____

_____

_____

_____

_____

Day #65: _____ (date)

Let's begin our intimate conversation today with ...

2 Chronicles 16:9a, "For the eyes of the LORD run to and fro throughout the whole earth, to show Himself strong on behalf of those whose heart is loyal to Him."

I love you!

Abba

_____

_____

_____

_____

_____

_____

_____

_____

_____

_____

_____

_____

_____

_____

_____

_____

_____

_____

_____

_____

_____

_____

_____

Day #66: _____ (date)

Let's begin our intimate conversation today with ...

2 Chronicles 20:15b, 17 (NIV), "This is what the LORD says to you: 'Do not be afraid or discouraged because of this vast army. For the battle is not yours, but God's. ... You will not have to fight this battle. Take up your positions; stand firm and see the deliverance the LORD will give you, O Judah and Jerusalem. Do not be afraid; do not be discouraged. Go out to face them tomorrow, and the LORD will be with you.'"

I love you!

Abba

_____

_____

_____

_____

_____

_____

_____

_____

_____

_____

_____

_____

_____

_____

_____

_____

_____

_____

_____

_____

_____

_____

_____

EZRA: THEME- RESTORATION

Two major messages emerge from Ezra: God's faithfulness and man's unfaithfulness. God keeps His promise to the unfaithful Israelites to deliver them from exile and return them home to the Promised Land. The constant reminder from this book is how easily God's people can become discouraged, even though God remains steadfastly faithful.

Day #67: _____ **(date)**

Let's begin our intimate conversation today with ...

Ezra 3:10-11, "When the builders laid the foundation of the temple of the LORD, the priests stood in their apparel with trumpets, and the Levites, the sons of Asaph, with cymbals, to praise the LORD, according to the ordinance of David king of Israel. And they sang responsively, praising and giving thanks to the LORD: 'For He is good, For His mercy endures forever toward Israel.' Then all the people shouted with a great shout, when they praised the LORD, because the foundation of the house of the LORD was laid."

I love you!

Abba

_____

_____

_____

_____

_____

_____

_____

_____

_____

_____

_____

_____

_____

Day #68: _____ **(date)**

Let's begin our intimate conversation today with ...

Ezra 4:4-5 (MSG), "So these people (of the land) started beating down the morale of the people of Judah, harassing them as they built. They even hired propagandists to sap their resolve. They kept this up for about fifteen years, throughout the lifetime of Cyrus king of Persia and on into the reign of Darius king of Persia."

I love you!

Abba

_____

_____

_____

_____

_____

_____

_____

_____

_____

_____

_____

_____

_____

_____

_____

_____

_____

_____

_____

_____

_____

Days #69 & #70: Rest and Reflect _____(dates)

Take some time to review what we shared over the past five days and record any new thoughts, feelings, insights, impressions, and responses. How did these intimate conversations impact you? How did they impact others as you interacted with them? What are you most grateful for?

I love you,

Abba

_____

_____

_____

_____

_____

_____

_____

_____

_____

_____

_____

_____

_____

_____

_____

_____

_____

_____

_____

_____

_____

_____

_____

Day #71: _____ (date)

Let's begin our intimate conversation today with ...

Ezra 7:28b (NIV), "Because the hand of the LORD my God was on me, I took courage and gathered leading men from Israel to go up with me."

I love you!

Abba

_____

_____

_____

_____

_____

_____

_____

_____

_____

_____

_____

_____

_____

_____

_____

_____

_____

_____

_____

_____

_____

_____

_____

_____

NEHEMIAH: THEME– RECONSTRUCTION

The Book of Nehemiah expresses the practical side of faith in God. Nehemiah led the rebuilding of the wall of Jerusalem. There was much opposition. This included mocking the wall-builders, threats, attacks, plots on Nehemiah's life, and false reports to the king. God's faithfulness to them is again highlighted. Despite all the opposition, the wall was built in fifty-two days.

Day #72: _____ **(date)**

Let's begin our intimate conversation today with ...

Nehemiah 2:17-20 (NIV), "Then I (Nehemiah) said to them, 'You see the trouble we are in: Jerusalem lies in ruins, and its gates have been burned with fire. Come, let us rebuild the wall of Jerusalem, and we will no longer be in disgrace.' I also told them about the gracious hand of my God upon me and what the king had said to me. They replied, 'Let us start rebuilding.' So they began this good work. But when Sanballat the Horonite, Tobiah the Ammonite official and Geshem the Arab heard about it, they mocked and ridiculed us. 'What is this you are doing?' they asked, 'Are you rebelling against the king?' I answered them by saying, 'The God of heaven will give us success. We his servants will start rebuilding, but as for you, you have no share in Jerusalem or any claim or historic right to it.'"

I love you!

Abba

_____

_____

_____

_____

_____

_____

_____

_____

_____

_____

_____

Day #73: _____ (date)

Let's begin our intimate conversation today with ...

Nehemiah 4:8-9 (NIV), "They all plotted together to come and fight against Jerusalem and stir up trouble against it. But we prayed to our God and posted a guard day and night to meet this threat."

I love you!

Abba

_____

_____

_____

_____

_____

_____

_____

_____

_____

_____

_____

_____

_____

_____

_____

_____

_____

_____

_____

_____

_____

_____

_____

Day #74: _____ (date)

Let's begin our intimate conversation today with ...

Nehemiah 4:15-20 (MSG), "Our enemies learned that we knew all about their plan and that God had frustrated it. And we went back to the wall and went to work. From then on half of my young men worked while the other half stood guard with lances, shields, bows, and mail armor. ... The common laborers held a tool in one hand and a spear in the other. Each of the builders had a sword strapped to his side as he worked. I kept the trumpeter at my side to sound the alert. ... When you hear the trumpet call, join us there; our God will fight for us.'"

I love you!

Abba

_____

_____

_____

_____

_____

_____

_____

_____

_____

_____

_____

_____

_____

_____

_____

_____

_____

_____

_____

_____

Day #75: _____ (date)

Let's begin our intimate conversation today with ...

Nehemiah 6:15-16 (MSG), "The wall was finished on the twenty-fifth day of Elul. It had taken fifty-two days. When all our enemies heard the news and all the surrounding nations saw it, our enemies totally lost their nerve. They knew that God was behind this work."

I love you!

Abba

_____

_____

_____

_____

_____

_____

_____

_____

_____

_____

_____

_____

_____

_____

_____

_____

_____

_____

_____

_____

_____

_____

_____

Days #76 & #77: Rest and Reflect _____ (dates)

Take some time to review what we shared over the past five days and record any new thoughts, feelings, insights, impressions, and responses. How did these intimate conversations impact you? How did they impact others as you interacted with them? What are you most grateful for?

I love you!

Abba

_____

_____

_____

_____

_____

_____

_____

_____

_____

_____

_____

_____

_____

_____

_____

_____

_____

_____

_____

_____

Day #78: _____ (date)

Let's begin our intimate conversation today with …

Nehemiah 8:10b, "…the joy of the LORD is your strength."

I love you!

Abba

_____

_____

_____

_____

_____

_____

_____

_____

_____

_____

_____

_____

_____

_____

_____

_____

_____

_____

_____

_____

_____

_____

_____

_____

_____

_____

_____

ESTHER: THEME— PROVIDENCE, PROTECTION AND PRESERVATION

The story of Esther is a classic struggle between good and evil. This book shows how God guides an unlikely Jewish woman, an orphan named Esther, to marry the Persian King, and courageously save her people from being completely destroyed. This book highlights God's sovereignty and deliverance.

Day #79: _____ (date)

Let's begin our intimate conversation today with ...

Esther 4:13, (Mordecai, Esther's Cousin and Guardian, responds to Esther after she tells him that she will die if she goes to the king uninvited). "And Mordecai told them to answer Esther: 'Do not think in your heart that you will escape in the king's palace any more than all the other Jews. For if you remain completely silent at this time, relief and deliverance will arise for the Jews from another place, but you and your father's house will perish. Yet who knows whether you have come to the kingdom for such a time as this?'"

I love you!

Abba

_____

_____

_____

_____

_____

_____

_____

_____

_____

_____

_____

_____

_____

_____

Day #80: _____ **(date)**

Let's begin our intimate conversation today with ...

Esther 4:15-16, "Then Esther told them to reply to Mordecai: 'Go, gather all the Jews who are present in Shushan, and fast for me; neither eat nor drink for three days, night or day. My maids and I will fast likewise. And so I will go to the king, which is against the law; and if I perish, I perish!'"

I love you!

Abba

_____

_____

_____

_____

_____

_____

_____

_____

_____

_____

_____

_____

_____

_____

_____

_____

_____

_____

_____

_____

_____

_____

Day #81: _____ (date)

Let's begin our intimate conversation today with ...

Esther 8:3-8 (MSG), "Then Esther again spoke to the king, falling at his feet, begging with tears to counter the evil of Haman the Agagite and revoke the plan that he had plotted against the Jews. The king extended his gold scepter to Esther. She got to her feet and stood before the king. She said, 'If it please the king and he regards me with favor and thinks this is right, and if he has any affection for me at all, let an order be written that cancels the bulletins authorizing the plan of Haman son of Hammedatha the Agagite to annihilate the Jews in all the king's provinces. How can I stand to see this catastrophe wipe out my people? How can I bear to stand by and watch the massacre of my own relatives?' ... 'So go ahead now and write whatever you decide on behalf of the Jews; then seal it with the signet ring.'"

I love you!

Abba

_____

_____

_____

_____

_____

_____

_____

_____

_____

_____

_____

_____

_____

_____

_____

_____

_____

_____

JOB: THEME— SUFFERING AND GOD'S SOVEREIGNTY

This book tells the story about God allowing Satan to strip Job, a righteous and rich man, of his wealth, family, and health. After suffering these losses, Job's faith is shaken and he struggles with why God would allow these losses to occur. The main message of this book is that God is sovereign and all-powerful despite what is happening in our lives. And, that God is always there for us, even when life doesn't make any sense. The book closes with Job experiencing a dramatic encounter with God, Job repenting, and God blessing him with more than he had before.

Day #82: _____ (date)

Let's begin our intimate conversation today with ...

Job 1:1, 14-15, 18, "There was a man in the land of Uz, whose name was Job; and that man was blameless and upright, and one who feared God and shunned evil. ... and a messenger came to Job and said, 'The oxen were plowing and the donkeys feeding beside them, when the Sabeans raided them and took them away— indeed they have killed the servants with the edge of the sword; and I alone have escaped to tell you! ...While he was still speaking, another also came and said, 'Your sons and daughters were eating and drinking wine in their oldest brother's house, and suddenly a great wind came from across the wilderness and struck the four corners of the house, and it fell on the young people, and they are dead; and I alone have escaped to tell you!'"

I love you!

Abba

_____

_____

_____

_____

_____

_____

_____

_____

Days #83 & #84: Rest and Reflect _____(dates)

Take some time to review what we shared over the past five days and record any new thoughts, feelings, insights, impressions, and responses. How did these intimate conversations impact you? How did they impact others as you interacted with them? What are you most grateful for?

I love you!

Abba

_____

_____

_____

_____

_____

_____

_____

_____

_____

_____

_____

_____

_____

_____

_____

_____

_____

_____

_____

_____

_____

_____

_____

Day #85: _____ (date)

Let's begin our intimate conversation today with …

Job 1:20-22, "Then Job arose, tore his robe, and shaved his head; and he fell to the ground and worshiped. And he said: 'Naked I came from my mother's womb, And naked shall I return there. The LORD gave, and the LORD has taken away; Blessed be the name of the LORD.' In all this Job did not sin nor charge God with wrong."

I love you!

Abba

_____

_____

_____

_____

_____

_____

_____

_____

_____

_____

_____

_____

_____

_____

_____

_____

_____

_____

_____

_____

_____

_____

_____

Day #86: _____ (date)

Let's begin our intimate conversation today with ...

Job 2:7-10 (MSG), "Satan left GOD and struck Job with terrible sores. Job was ulcers and scabs from head to foot. They itched and oozed so badly that he took a piece of broken pottery to scrape himself, then went and sat on a trash heap, among the ashes. His wife said, 'Still holding on to your precious integrity, are you? Curse God and be done with it!' He told her, 'You're talking like an empty-headed fool. We take the good days from God—why not also the bad days?' Not once through all this did Job sin. He said nothing against God."

I love you!

Abba

_____

_____

_____

_____

_____

_____

_____

_____

_____

_____

_____

_____

_____

_____

_____

_____

_____

_____

_____

_____

_____

_____

Day #87: _____ (date)

Let's begin our intimate conversation today with ...

Job 3:1a (MSG); 19:7 (NIV), "Then Job broke the silence. He spoke up and cursed his fate: 'Obliterate the day I was born.' ... 'Though I cry, 'I've been wronged!' I get no response; though I call for help, there is no justice.'"

I love you!

Abba

_____

_____

_____

_____

_____

_____

_____

_____

_____

_____

_____

_____

_____

_____

_____

_____

_____

_____

_____

_____

_____

_____

_____

Day #88: _____ **(date)**

Let's begin our intimate conversation today with …

Job 38:1-7 (NIV), "Then the LORD answered Job out of the storm. He said: 'Who is this that darkens my counsel with words without knowledge? Brace yourself like a man; I will question you, and you shall answer me. Where were you when I laid the earth's foundation? Tell me, if you understand. Who marked off its dimensions? Surely you know! Who stretched a measuring line across it? On what were it's footings set, or who laid its cornerstone—while the morning stars sang together and all the angels shouted for joy?'"

I love you!

Abba

_____

_____

_____

_____

_____

_____

_____

_____

_____

_____

_____

_____

_____

_____

_____

_____

_____

_____

_____

_____

Day #89: _____ (date)

Let's begin our intimate conversation today with ...

Job 42:5-6,10 (NIV), "'My ears had heard of you but now my eyes have seen you. Therefore I despise myself and repent in dust and ashes.' ... After Job had prayed for his friends, the LORD made him prosperous again and gave him twice as much as he had before."

I love you!

Abba

_____

_____

_____

_____

_____

_____

_____

_____

_____

_____

_____

_____

_____

_____

_____

_____

_____

_____

_____

_____

_____

_____

Day #90 & #91: Rest and Reflect _____ **(dates)**

Take some time to review what we shared over the past five days and record any new thoughts, feelings, insights, impressions, and responses. How did these intimate conversations impact you? How did they impact others as you interacted with them? What are you most grateful for?

I love you!

Abba

_____

_____

_____

_____

_____

_____

_____

_____

_____

_____

_____

_____

_____

_____

_____

_____

_____

_____

_____

_____

_____

_____

_____

PSALMS: THEME- COMMUNION WITH GOD IN PRAISE, WORSHIP, AND PRAYER

Psalms is the longest book in the Bible. It is the compilation of several ancient collections of Hebrew songs, prayers, petitions, meditations, instructions, laments, historical anthems, and poems for use in congregational worship and in private devotions. Approximately half of the Old Testament references to the Messiah quoted by New Testament writers are from the Book of Psalms. Throughout the centuries the Psalms have been a source of personal inspiration and spiritual strength.

Day #92: _____ **(date)**

Let's begin our intimate conversation today with ...

Psalm 1:1-3 (NIV), "Blessed is the man who does not walk in the counsel of the wicked or stand in the way of sinners or sit in the seat of mockers. But his delight is in the law of the LORD, and on his law he meditates day and night. He is like a tree planted by streams of water, which yields its fruit in season and whose leaf does not wither. Whatever he does prospers."

I love you!

Abba

_____

_____

_____

_____

_____

_____

_____

_____

_____

_____

_____

_____

_____

Day #93: _____ **(date)**

Let's begin our intimate conversation today with ...

Psalm 16:11, "You will show me the path of life; In Your presence is fullness of joy; At Your right hand are pleasures forevermore."

I love you!

Abba

_____

_____

_____

_____

_____

_____

_____

_____

_____

_____

_____

_____

_____

_____

_____

_____

_____

_____

_____

_____

_____

_____

_____

Day #94: _____ **(date)**

Let's begin our intimate conversation today with ...

Psalm 18:1-3a, "I WILL love You, O LORD, my strength. The LORD is my rock and my fortress and my deliverer; My God, my strength, in whom I will trust; My shield and the horn of my salvation, my stronghold. I will call upon the LORD, who is worthy to be praised."

I love you!

Abba

_____

_____

_____

_____

_____

_____

_____

_____

_____

_____

_____

_____

_____

_____

_____

_____

_____

_____

_____

_____

_____

_____

_____

Day #95: _____ **(date)**

Let's begin our intimate conversation today with ...

Psalm 19:7-8 (MSG), "The revelation of GOD is whole and pulls our lives together. The signposts of GOD are clear and point out the right road. The life-maps of GOD are right, showing the way to joy."

I love you!

Abba

_____

_____

_____

_____

_____

_____

_____

_____

_____

_____

_____

_____

_____

_____

_____

_____

_____

_____

_____

_____

_____

_____

_____

_____

_____

Day #96: _____ (date)

Let's begin our intimate conversation today with ...

Psalm 23:1, "The LORD is my shepherd; I shall not want."

I love you!

Abba

_____

_____

_____

_____

_____

_____

_____

_____

_____

_____

_____

_____

_____

_____

_____

_____

_____

_____

_____

_____

_____

_____

_____

_____

Days #97 & #98: Rest and Reflect _____ (dates)

Take some time to review what we shared over the past five days and record any new thoughts, feelings, insights, impressions, and responses. How did these intimate conversations impact you? How did they impact others as you interacted with them? What are you most grateful for?

I love you!

Abba

_____

_____

_____

_____

_____

_____

_____

_____

_____

_____

_____

_____

_____

_____

_____

_____

_____

_____

_____

_____

_____

_____

_____

Day #99: _____ (date)

Let's begin our intimate conversation today with ...

Psalm 25:4-5, "Show me Your ways, O LORD; Teach me Your paths. Lead me in Your truth and teach me, for You are the God of my salvation; On You I wait all the day."

I love you!

Abba

_____

_____

_____

_____

_____

_____

_____

_____

_____

_____

_____

_____

_____

_____

_____

_____

_____

_____

_____

_____

_____

_____

_____

_____

_____

Day #100: _____ (date)

Let's begin our intimate conversation today with ...

Psalm 27:14, "Wait on the LORD; Be of good courage, And He shall strengthen your heart; Wait, I say, on the LORD!"

I love you!

Abba

_____

_____

_____

_____

_____

_____

_____

_____

_____

_____

_____

_____

_____

_____

_____

_____

_____

_____

_____

_____

_____

_____

_____

_____

_____

Day #101: _____ (date)

Let's begin our intimate conversation today with ...

Psalm 30:11-12, "You have turned for me my mourning into dancing; You have put off my sackcloth and clothed me with gladness, To the end that my glory may sing praise to You and not be silent. O LORD my God, I will give thanks to You forever."

I love you!

Abba

_____

_____

_____

_____

_____

_____

_____

_____

_____

_____

_____

_____

_____

_____

_____

_____

_____

_____

_____

_____

_____

_____

_____

_____

_____

Day #102: _____ (date)

Let's begin our intimate conversation today with ...

Psalm 46:10, "Be still, and know that I am God; I will be exalted among the nations, I will be exalted in the earth!"

I love you!

Abba

_____

_____

_____

_____

_____

_____

_____

_____

_____

_____

_____

_____

_____

_____

_____

_____

_____

_____

_____

_____

_____

_____

_____

_____

_____

_____

Day #103: _____ (date)

Let's begin our intimate conversations today with ...

Psalm 51:10 (NIV), "Create in me a pure heart, O God, and renew a steadfast spirit within me."

I love you!

Abba

_____

_____

_____

_____

_____

_____

_____

_____

_____

_____

_____

_____

_____

_____

_____

_____

_____

_____

_____

_____

_____

_____

_____

_____

_____

Days #104 & #105: Rest and Reflect _____(dates)

Take some time to review what we shared over the past five days and record any new thoughts, feelings, insights, impressions, and responses. How did these intimate conversations impact you? How did they impact others as you interacted with them? What are you most grateful for?

I love you!

Abba

_____

_____

_____

_____

_____

_____

_____

_____

_____

_____

_____

_____

_____

_____

_____

_____

_____

_____

_____

_____

_____

_____

Day #106: _____ (date)

Let's begin our intimate conversation today with ...

Psalm 56:8-9, "You number my wanderings; Put my tears into Your bottle; Are they not in Your book? When I cry out to You, Then my enemies will turn back; This I know, because God is for me."

I love you!

Abba

_____

_____

_____

_____

_____

_____

_____

_____

_____

_____

_____

_____

_____

_____

_____

_____

_____

_____

_____

_____

_____

Day #107: _____ (date)

Let's begin our intimate conversation today with ...

Psalm 100:1-5, "Make a joyful shout to the LORD, all you lands! Serve the LORD with gladness; Come before His presence with singing. Know that the LORD, He is God; It is He who has made us, and not we ourselves; We are His people and the sheep of His pasture. Enter into His gates with thanksgiving, and into His courts with praise. Be thankful to Him and bless His name. For the LORD is good; His mercy is everlasting, And His truth endures to all generations."

I love you!

Abba

_____

_____

_____

_____

_____

_____

_____

_____

_____

_____

_____

_____

_____

_____

_____

_____

_____

_____

_____

_____

_____

Day #108: _____ **(date)**

Let's begin our intimate conversation today with ...

Psalm 119:105, "Your word is a lamp to my feet And a light to my path."

I love you!

Abba

_____

_____

_____

_____

_____

_____

_____

_____

_____

_____

_____

_____

_____

_____

_____

_____

_____

_____

_____

_____

_____

_____

_____

_____

_____

_____

Day #109: _____ **(date)**

Let's begin our intimate conversation today with ...

Psalm 139:13-14 (NIV), "For you created my inmost being; you knit me together in my mother's womb. I praise you because I am fearfully and wonderfully made; your works are wonderful, I know that full well."

I love you!

Abba

_____

_____

_____

_____

_____

_____

_____

_____

_____

_____

_____

_____

_____

_____

_____

_____

_____

_____

_____

_____

_____

_____

_____

Day #110: _____ **(date)**

Let's begin our intimate conversation today with ...

Psalm 150:6, "Let everything that has breath praise the LORD. Praise the LORD!"

I love you!

Abba

_____

_____

_____

_____

_____

_____

_____

_____

_____

_____

_____

_____

_____

_____

_____

_____

_____

_____

_____

_____

_____

_____

_____

_____

Days #111 & #112: Rest and Reflect _____(dates)

Take some time to review what we shared over the past five days and record any new thoughts, feelings, insights, impressions, and responses. How did these intimate conversations impact you? How did they impact others as you interacted with them? What are you most grateful for?

I love you!

Abba

_____

_____

_____

_____

_____

_____

_____

_____

_____

_____

_____

_____

_____

_____

_____

_____

_____

_____

_____

_____

_____

_____

PROVERBS: THEME— PRACTICAL WISDOM

This book contains practical advice in the form of proverbs. A proverb is a short, concise sentence that conveys moral truth. The Proverbs' purpose is to help people live wisely and productively. This book's wisdom is as relevant today as when it was written over two thousand years ago.

Day #113: _____ **(date)**

Let's begin our intimate conversation today with ...

Proverbs 1:7, "The fear of the LORD is the beginning of knowledge, But fools despise wisdom and instruction."

I love you!

Abba

_____

_____

_____

_____

_____

_____

_____

_____

_____

_____

_____

_____

_____

_____

_____

_____

_____

_____

_____

Day #114: _____ *(date)*

Let's begin our intimate conversation today with ...

Proverbs 3:5-8 (MSG), "Trust GOD from the bottom of your heart; don't try to figure out everything on your own. Listen for GOD's voice in everything you do, everywhere you go; he's the one who will keep you on track. Don't assume that you know it all. Run to GOD! Run from evil! Your body will glow with health, your very bones will vibrate with life."

I love you!

Abba

_____

_____

_____

_____

_____

_____

_____

_____

_____

_____

_____

_____

_____

_____

_____

_____

_____

_____

_____

_____

_____

Day #115: _____ ***(date)***

Let's begin our intimate conversation today with ...

Proverbs 4:23 (NIV), "Above all else, guard your heart, for it is the wellspring of life."

I love you!

Abba

_____

_____

_____

_____

_____

_____

_____

_____

_____

_____

_____

_____

_____

_____

_____

_____

_____

_____

_____

_____

_____

_____

_____

Day #116: _____ **(date)**

Let's begin our intimate conversation today with ...

Proverbs 8:17, "I love those who love me, And those who seek me diligently will find me."

I love you!

Abba

_____

_____

_____

_____

_____

_____

_____

_____

_____

_____

_____

_____

_____

_____

_____

_____

_____

_____

_____

_____

_____

_____

_____

Day #117: _____ (date)

Let's begin our intimate conversation today with ...

Proverbs 11:14, "Where there is no counsel, the people fall; But in the multitude of counselors there is safety."

I love you!

Abba

_____

_____

_____

_____

_____

_____

_____

_____

_____

_____

_____

_____

_____

_____

_____

_____

_____

_____

_____

_____

_____

_____

_____

Days #118 & #119: Rest and Reflect. _____(dates)

Take some time to review what we shared over the past five days and record any new thoughts, feelings, insights, impressions, and responses. How did these intimate conversations impact you? How did they impact others as you interacted with them? What are you most grateful for?

I love you!

Abba

_____

_____

_____

_____

_____

_____

_____

_____

_____

_____

_____

_____

_____

_____

_____

_____

_____

_____

_____

_____

_____

_____

Day #120: _____ (date)

Let's begin our intimate conversation today with ...

Proverbs 13:20 (NIV), "He who walks with the wise grows wise, but a companion of fools suffers harm."

I love you!

Abba

_____

_____

_____

_____

_____

_____

_____

_____

_____

_____

_____

_____

_____

_____

_____

_____

_____

_____

_____

_____

_____

_____

_____

_____

Day #121: _____ (date)

Let's begin our intimate conversation today with ...

Proverbs 15:1; 16:24 (NIV), "A gentle answer turns away wrath, but a harsh word stirs up anger."... "Pleasant words are a honeycomb, sweet to the soul and healing to the bones."

I love you!

Abba

_____

_____

_____

_____

_____

_____

_____

_____

_____

_____

_____

_____

_____

_____

_____

_____

_____

_____

_____

_____

_____

_____

Day #122: _____ (date)

Let's begin our intimate conversation today with ...

Proverbs 16:18, "Pride goes before destruction, And a haughty spirit before a fall."

I love you!

Abba

_____

_____

_____

_____

_____

_____

_____

_____

_____

_____

_____

_____

_____

_____

_____

_____

_____

_____

_____

_____

_____

_____

_____

Day #123: _____ (date)

Let's begin our intimate conversation today with ...

Proverbs 17:22 (NIV), "A cheerful heart is good medicine, but a crushed spirit dries up the bones."

I love you!

Abba

_____

_____

_____

_____

_____

_____

_____

_____

_____

_____

_____

_____

_____

_____

_____

_____

_____

_____

_____

_____

_____

_____

_____

Day #124: _____ (date)

Let's begin our intimate conversations today with ...

Proverbs 18:13, "He who answers a matter before he hears it, It is folly and shame to him."

I love you!

Abba

_____

_____

_____

_____

_____

_____

_____

_____

_____

_____

_____

_____

_____

_____

_____

_____

_____

_____

_____

_____

_____

_____

_____

_____

_____

_____

Days #125 & #126: Rest and Reflect _____(dates)

Take some time to review what we shared over the past five days and record any new thoughts, feelings, insights, impressions, and responses. How did these intimate conversations impact you? How did they impact others as you interacted with them? What are you most grateful for?

I love you!

Abba

_____

_____

_____

_____

_____

_____

_____

_____

_____

_____

_____

_____

_____

_____

_____

_____

_____

_____

_____

_____

_____

_____

_____

Day #127: _____ **(date)**

Let's begin our intimate conversation today with ...

Proverbs 18:21 (MSG), "Words kill, words give life; they're either poison or fruit—you choose."

I love you!

Abba

_____

_____

_____

_____

_____

_____

_____

_____

_____

_____

_____

_____

_____

_____

_____

_____

_____

_____

_____

_____

_____

_____

_____

_____

_____

_____

Day #128: _____ (date)

Let's begin our intimate conversation today with ...

Proverbs 19:20 (MSG), "Take good counsel and accept correction—that's the way to live wisely and well."

I love you!

Abba

_____

_____

_____

_____

_____

_____

_____

_____

_____

_____

_____

_____

_____

_____

_____

_____

_____

_____

_____

_____

_____

_____

_____

Day #129: _____ **(date)**

Let's begin our intimate conversation today with ...

Proverbs 23:7a; 27:19, "For as he thinks in his heart, so is he." ... "As in water face reflects face, So a man's heart reveals the man."

I love you!

Abba

_____

_____

_____

_____

_____

_____

_____

_____

_____

_____

_____

_____

_____

_____

_____

_____

_____

_____

_____

_____

_____

_____

_____

_____

_____

Day #130: _____ (date)

Let's begin our intimate conversation today with ...

Proverbs 28:13 (NIV), "He who conceals his sins does not prosper, but whoever confesses and renounces them finds mercy."

I love you!

Abba

_____

_____

_____

_____

_____

_____

_____

_____

_____

_____

_____

_____

_____

_____

_____

_____

_____

_____

_____

_____

_____

_____

_____

_____

_____

Day #131: _____ (date)

Let's begin our intimate conversation with ...

Proverbs 30:5, "Every word of God is pure; He is a shield to those who put their trust in Him."

I love you!

Abba

_____

_____

_____

_____

_____

_____

_____

_____

_____

_____

_____

_____

_____

_____

_____

_____

_____

_____

_____

_____

_____

_____

_____

_____

_____

Days #132 & #133: Rest and Reflect _____(dates)

Take some time to review what we shared over the past five days and record any new thoughts, feelings, insights, impressions, and responses. How did these intimate conversations impact you? How did they impact others as you interacted with them? What are you most grateful for?

I love you!

Abba

_____

_____

_____

_____

_____

_____

_____

_____

_____

_____

_____

_____

_____

_____

_____

_____

_____

_____

_____

_____

_____

_____

_____

_____

_____

ECCLESIASTES: THEME- QUEST FOR TRUE VALUE IN LIFE

In this book the author explores a search for something of true value as he struggles with trying to find meaning and purpose in life. His hopeful conclusion is that in this fallen world a person is able to find ultimate meaning and purpose through a relationship with God.

Day #134: _____ **(date)**

Let's begin our intimate conversation with ...

Ecclesiastes 1:1-3 (NIV), "The words of the Teacher, son of David, king in Jerusalem: 'Meaningless! Meaningless!' says the Teacher. 'Utterly meaningless! Everything is meaningless.' What does man gain from all his labor at which he toils under the sun?"

I love you!

Abba

_____

_____

_____

_____

_____

_____

_____

_____

_____

_____

_____

_____

_____

_____

_____

_____

_____

_____

Day #135: _____ **(date)**

Let's begin our intimate conversation today with ...

Ecclesiastes 2:10-11 (NIV), "I denied myself nothing my eyes desired; I refused my heart no pleasure. My heart took delight in all my work, and this was the reward for all my labor. Yet when I surveyed all that my hands had done and what I had toiled to achieve, everything was meaningless, a chasing after the wind; nothing was gained under the sun."

I love you!

Abba

_____

_____

_____

_____

_____

_____

_____

_____

_____

_____

_____

_____

_____

_____

_____

_____

_____

_____

_____

_____

_____

_____

Day #136: _____ (date)

Let's begin our intimate conversation today with ...

Ecclesiastes 3:1-2, 4, "To everything there is a season, A time for every purpose under heaven: A time to be born, And a time to die; A time to plant, And a time to pluck what is planted; ... A time to weep, And a time to laugh; A time to mourn, And a time to dance."

I love you!

Abba

_____

_____

_____

_____

_____

_____

_____

_____

_____

_____

_____

_____

_____

_____

_____

_____

_____

_____

_____

_____

_____

_____

_____

_____

_____

Day #137: _____ (date)

Let's begin our intimate conversation today with ...

Ecclesiastes 4:9-10, 12 (NIV), "Two are better than one, because they have a good return for their work: If one falls down, his friend can help him up. But pity the man who falls and has no one to help him up! ...Though one may be overpowered, two can defend themselves. A cord of three strands is not quickly broken."

I love you!

Abba

_____

_____

_____

_____

_____

_____

_____

_____

_____

_____

_____

_____

_____

_____

_____

_____

_____

_____

_____

_____

_____

_____

Day #138: _____ (date)

Let's begin our intimate conversations today with ...

Ecclesiastes 12:13-14 (NIV), "Now all has been heard; here is the conclusion of the matter: Fear God and keep his commandments, for this is the whole duty of man. For God will bring every deed into judgment, including every hidden thing, whether it is good or evil."

I love you!

Abba

_____

_____

_____

_____

_____

_____

_____

_____

_____

_____

_____

_____

_____

_____

_____

_____

_____

_____

_____

_____

_____

_____

_____

_____

Days #139 & #140: Rest and Reflect _____(dates)

Take some time to review what we shared over the past five days and record any new thoughts, feelings, insights, impressions, and responses. How did these intimate conversations impact you? How did they impact others as you interacted with them? What are you most grateful for?

I love you!

Abba

_____

_____

_____

_____

_____

_____

_____

_____

_____

_____

_____

_____

_____

_____

_____

_____

_____

_____

_____

_____

_____

_____

_____

_____

SONG OF SOLOMON: THEME— AUTHENTIC LOVE

"Love" is the key word in this book. It focuses on the passionate love between a man and a woman and celebrates marriage in light of a covenant love. Covenant love is also the basis of the relationship between God and man.

Day #141: _____ (date)

Let's begin our intimate conversation today with ...

Song of Solomon 2:4-5, "He brought me to the banqueting house, And his banner over me was love. Sustain me with cakes of raisins, Refresh me with apples, For I am lovesick."

I love you!

Abba

_____

_____

_____

_____

_____

_____

_____

_____

_____

_____

_____

_____

_____

_____

_____

_____

_____

_____

Day #142: _____ (date)

Let's begin our intimate conversation today with ...

Song of Solomon 2:10,14, "My beloved spoke, and said to me: 'Rise up, my love, my fair one, And come away. ... O my dove, in the clefts of the rock, In the secret places of the cliff, Let me see your face, Let me hear your voice; For your voice is sweet, And your face is lovely.'"

I love you!

Abba

_____

_____

_____

_____

_____

_____

_____

_____

_____

_____

_____

_____

_____

_____

_____

_____

_____

_____

_____

_____

_____

_____

_____

_____

Day #143: _____ **(date)**

Let's begin our intimate conversations today with ...

Song of Solomon 7:10, "I am my beloved's, And his desire is toward me."

I love you!

Abba

_____

_____

_____

_____

_____

_____

_____

_____

_____

_____

_____

_____

_____

_____

_____

_____

_____

_____

_____

_____

_____

_____

_____

_____

_____

_____

Day #144: _____ (date)

Let's begin our intimate conversation today with ...

Song of Solomon 8:7 (MSG), "Flood waters can't drown love, torrents of rain can't put it out. Love can't be bought, love can't be sold..."

I love you!

Abba

_____

_____

_____

_____

_____

_____

_____

_____

_____

_____

_____

_____

_____

_____

_____

_____

_____

_____

_____

_____

_____

_____

ISAIAH: THEME– SALVATION

In this book Isaiah warns God's people about the consequences of judgment if they continue their disobedient ways. But, the greatest purpose of this book was to give hope to the faithful ones. This book is full of promises of restoration and redemption through the coming of the Messiah, of salvation for all nations, and the triumph of God's purposes in spite of sufferings along the way.

Day #145: _____ (date)

Let's begin our intimate conversation today with …

Isaiah 7:14; 9:6 (NIV), "Therefore the Lord himself will give you a sign: The virgin will be with child and will give birth to a son, and will call him Immanuel." … "For to us a child is born, to us a son is given, and the government will be on his shoulders. And he will be called Wonderful Counselor, Mighty God, Everlasting Father, Prince of Peace."

I love you!

Abba

_____

_____

_____

_____

_____

_____

_____

_____

_____

_____

_____

_____

_____

_____

_____

_____

Days #146 & #147: Rest and Reflect _____(dates)

Take some time to review what we shared over the past five days and record any new thoughts, feelings, insights, impressions, and responses. How did these intimate conversations impact you? How did they impact others as you interacted with them? What are you most grateful for?

I love you!

Abba

_____

_____

_____

_____

_____

_____

_____

_____

_____

_____

_____

_____

_____

_____

_____

_____

_____

_____

_____

_____

_____

_____

_____

Day #148: _____ **(date)**

Let's begin our intimate conversation today with ...

Isaiah 26:3-4, "You will keep him in perfect peace, Whose mind is stayed on You, Because he trusts in You. Trust in the LORD forever, For in YAH, the LORD, is everlasting strength."

I love you!

Abba

_____

_____

_____

_____

_____

_____

_____

_____

_____

_____

_____

_____

_____

_____

_____

_____

_____

_____

_____

_____

_____

_____

_____

Day #149: _____ (date)

Let's begin our intimate conversation today with ...

Isaiah 40:31, "But those who wait on the LORD Shall renew their strength; They shall mount up with wings like eagles, They shall run and not be weary, They shall walk and not faint."

I love you!

Abba

_____

_____

_____

_____

_____

_____

_____

_____

_____

_____

_____

_____

_____

_____

_____

_____

_____

_____

_____

_____

_____

_____

Day #150: _____ (date)

Let's begin our intimate conversation today with ...

Isaiah 41:10, "Fear not, for I am with you; Be not dismayed, for I am your God. I will strengthen you, Yes, I will help you, I will uphold you with My righteous right hand."

I love you!

Abba

_____

_____

_____

_____

_____

_____

_____

_____

_____

_____

_____

_____

_____

_____

_____

_____

_____

_____

_____

_____

_____

_____

_____

Day #151: _____ (date)

Let's begin our intimate conversation today with ...

Isaiah 54:17, "'No weapon formed against you shall prosper, And every tongue which rises against you in judgment You shall condemn. This is the heritage of the servants of the LORD, And their righteousness is from Me,' Says the LORD."

I love you!

Abba

_____

_____

_____

_____

_____

_____

_____

_____

_____

_____

_____

_____

_____

_____

_____

_____

_____

_____

_____

_____

_____

_____

Day #152: _____ (date)

Let's begin our intimate conversation today with ...

Isaiah 55:8-9, "'For My thoughts are not your thoughts, Nor are your ways My ways.' says the LORD. 'For as the heavens are higher than the earth, So are My ways higher than your ways, And My thoughts than your thoughts.'"

I love you!

Abba

_____

_____

_____

_____

_____

_____

_____

_____

_____

_____

_____

_____

_____

_____

_____

_____

_____

_____

_____

_____

_____

_____

Days #153 & #154: Rest and Reflect _____ (dates)

Take some time to review what we shared over the past five days and record any new thoughts, feelings, insights, impressions, and responses. How did these intimate conversations impact you? How did they impact others as you interacted with them? What are you most grateful for?

I love you!

Abba

_____

_____

_____

_____

_____

_____

_____

_____

_____

_____

_____

_____

_____

_____

_____

_____

_____

_____

_____

_____

_____

_____

Day #155: _____ (date)

Let's begin our intimate conversation today with ...

Isaiah 58:11 (NIV), "The LORD will guide you always; he will satisfy your needs in a sun-scorched land and will strengthen your frame. You will be like a well-watered garden, like a spring whose waters never fail."

I love you!

Abba

_____

_____

_____

_____

_____

_____

_____

_____

_____

_____

_____

_____

_____

_____

_____

_____

_____

_____

_____

_____

_____

_____

Day #156: _____ **(date)**

Let's begin our intimate conversation today with ...

Isaiah 61:1-3 (MSG), "The Spirit of GOD, the Master, is on me because GOD anointed me. He sent me to preach good news to the poor, heal the heartbroken, Announce freedom to all captives, pardon all prisoners. GOD sent me to announce the year of his grace—a celebration of God's destruction of our enemies—and to comfort all who mourn. To care for the needs of all who mourn in Zion, give them bouquets of roses instead of ashes, Messages of joy instead of news of doom, a praising heart instead of a languid spirit. Rename them 'Oaks of Righteousness' planted by GOD to display his glory."

I love you!

Abba

_____

_____

_____

_____

_____

_____

_____

_____

_____

_____

_____

_____

_____

_____

_____

_____

_____

_____

_____

_____

_____

JEREMIAH: THEME— JUDGMENT

In spite of Jeremiah's message of doom, his scathing rebuke of the rulers, priests and false prophets, nobody listened. Although Jeremiah shared this tough message, when the disasters he had predicted started to happen, he began to speak about hope for the future. Jeremiah's message is timeless: sin must always be punished, but true repentance brings restoration.

Day #157: _____ **(date)**

Let's begin our intimate conversation today with ...

Jeremiah 9:23-24 (NIV), "This is what the LORD says: 'Let not the wise man boast of his wisdom or the strong man boast of his strength or the rich man boast of his riches, but let him who boasts boast about this: that he understands and knows me, that I am the LORD, who exercises kindness, justice and righteousness on earth, for in these I delight,' declares the LORD."

I love you!

Abba

_____

_____

_____

_____

_____

_____

_____

_____

_____

_____

_____

_____

_____

_____

_____

_____

_____

Day #158: _____ **(date)**

Let's begin our intimate conversation today with …

Jeremiah 17:5-6 (NIV), "This is what the LORD says: 'Cursed is the one who trusts in man, who depends on flesh for his strength and whose heart turns away from the LORD. He will be like a bush in the wastelands; he will not see prosperity when it comes. He will dwell in the parched places of the desert, in a salt land where no one lives.'"

I love you!

Abba

_____

_____

_____

_____

_____

_____

_____

_____

_____

_____

_____

_____

_____

_____

_____

_____

_____

_____

_____

_____

_____

_____

_____

Day #159: _____ (date)

Let's begin our intimate conversation today with ...

Jeremiah 29:10-13, "For thus says the LORD: 'After seventy years are completed at Babylon, I will visit you and perform My good word toward you, and cause you to return to this place. For I know the thoughts that I think toward you,' says the LORD, 'thoughts of peace and not of evil, to give you a future and a hope. Then you will call upon Me and go and pray to Me, and I will listen to you. And you will seek Me and find Me, when you search for Me with all your heart.'"

I love you!

Abba

_____

_____

_____

_____

_____

_____

_____

_____

_____

_____

_____

_____

_____

_____

_____

_____

_____

_____

_____

_____

_____

_____

_____

Days #160 & #161: Rest and Reflect _____(dates)

Take some time to review what we shared over the past five days and record any new thoughts, feelings, insights, impressions, and responses. How did these intimate conversations impact you? How did they impact others as you interacted with them? What are you most grateful for?

I love you!

Abba

_____

_____

_____

_____

_____

_____

_____

_____

_____

_____

_____

_____

_____

_____

_____

_____

_____

_____

_____

_____

_____

_____

_____

Day #162: _____ **(date)**

Let's begin our intimate conversation today with ...

Jeremiah 32:17, "Ah, Lord GOD! Behold, You have made the heavens and the earth by Your great power and outstretched arm. There is nothing too hard for You."

I love you!

Abba

_____

_____

_____

_____

_____

_____

_____

_____

_____

_____

_____

_____

_____

_____

_____

_____

_____

_____

_____

_____

_____

_____

LAMENTATIONS: THEME- SIN BRINGS CHAOS AND SUFFERING

In this book Jeremiah, known as the "weeping prophet", agonizes over the destruction of Jerusalem, the people's suffering and exile. This book also shows that the main purpose of God's divine discipline is His merciful attempt to draw His people back to Himself.

Day #163: _____ **(date)**

Let's begin our intimate conversation today with ...

Lamentations 1:18 (NIV), "The LORD is righteous, yet I rebelled against his command. Listen, all you peoples; look upon my suffering. My young men and maidens have gone into exile."

I love you!

Abba

_____

_____

_____

_____

_____

_____

_____

_____

_____

_____

_____

_____

_____

_____

_____

_____

_____

_____

Day #164: _____ (date)

Let's begin our intimate conversation today with ...

Lamentations 3:22-23 (NIV), "Because of the LORD's great love we are not consumed, for his compassions never fail. They are new every morning; great is your faithfulness."

I love you!

Abba

_____

_____

_____

_____

_____

_____

_____

_____

_____

_____

_____

_____

_____

_____

_____

_____

_____

_____

_____

_____

_____

_____

Day #165: _____ **(date)**

Let's begin our intimate conversation today with ...

Lamentations 3:40-41, "Let us search out and examine our ways, And turn back to the LORD; Let us lift our hearts and hands To God in heaven."

I love you!

Abba

_____

_____

_____

_____

_____

_____

_____

_____

_____

_____

_____

_____

_____

_____

_____

_____

_____

_____

_____

_____

_____

_____

_____

_____

_____

Day #166: _____ (date)

Let's begin our intimate conversation today with ...

Lamentations 5:21, "Turn us back to You, O LORD, and we will be restored; Renew our days as of old."

I love you!

Abba

_____

_____

_____

_____

_____

_____

_____

_____

_____

_____

_____

_____

_____

_____

_____

_____

_____

_____

_____

_____

_____

_____

_____

_____

Days #167 & #168: Rest and Reflect _____(dates)

Take some time to review what we shared over the past five days and record any new thoughts, feelings, insights, impressions, and responses. How did these intimate conversations impact you? How did they impact others as you interacted with them? What are you most grateful for?

I love you!

Abba

_____

_____

_____

_____

_____

_____

_____

_____

_____

_____

_____

_____

_____

_____

_____

_____

_____

_____

_____

_____

_____

_____

_____

_____

EZEKIEL: THEME- DESTRUCTION OF JERUSALEM AND ITS RESTORATION

Ezekiel wrote this book to the disillusioned and demoralized exiles in Babylon. He challenged them to acknowledge that each person must accept personal responsibility for God's judgment and their exile to Babylon. The book concludes with a message of hope as Ezekiel proclaims the faithfulness of God and the restoration of the people and land of Israel.

Day #169: _____ (date)

Let's begin our intimate conversation today with ...

Ezekiel 18:30-32 (NIV), "'Therefore, O house of Israel, I will judge you, each one according to his ways,' declares the Sovereign LORD. 'Repent! Turn away from all your offenses; then sin will not be your downfall. Rid yourselves of all the offenses you have committed, and get a new heart and a new spirit. Why will you die, O house of Israel? For I take no pleasure in the death of anyone,' declares the Sovereign LORD. 'Repent and live!'"

I love you!

Abba

Day #170: _____ (date)

Let's begin our intimate conversation today with ...

Ezekiel 36:24-28 (MSG), "'For here's what I'm going to do: I'm going to take you out of these countries, gather you from all over, and bring you back to your own land. I'll pour pure water over you and scrub you clean. I'll give you a new heart, put a new spirit in you. I'll remove the stone heart from your body and replace it with a heart that's God-willed, not self-willed. I'll put my Spirit in you and make it possible for you to do what I tell you and live by my commands. You'll once again live in the land I gave your ancestors. You'll be my people! I'll be your God!'"

I love you!

Abba

_____

_____

_____

_____

_____

_____

_____

_____

_____

_____

_____

_____

_____

_____

_____

_____

_____

_____

_____

_____

DANIEL: THEME- THE SOVEREIGNTY OF GOD

Daniel contains the record of the Jews' seventy-year captivity in Babylon. Within this book, Daniel and his three friends, Shadrach, Meshach, and Abed-Nego, displayed an uncompromising commitment to God that provided opportunities for Him to display His power on their behalf.

The second half of the book gives understanding to a believer's future, assuring us that history is under God's sovereign control.

Day #171: _____ (date)

Let's begin our intimate conversation today with ...

Daniel 3:4-6, "Then a herald cried aloud: 'To you it is commanded, O peoples, nations, and languages, that at the time you hear the sound of the horn, flute, harp, lyre, and psaltery, in symphony with all kinds of music, you shall fall down and worship the gold image that King Nebuchadnezzar has set up; and whoever does not fall down and worship shall be cast immediately into the midst of a burning fiery furnace.'"

I love you!

Abba

_____

_____

_____

_____

_____

_____

_____

_____

_____

_____

_____

_____

_____

_____

Day #172: _____ (date)

Let's begin our intimate conversation today with ...

Daniel 3:14, 16-18 (NIV), "and Nebuchadnezzar said to them, 'Is it true, Shadrach, Meshach and Abednego, that you do not serve my gods or worship the image of gold I have set up?' ...Shadrach, Meshach, and Abednego replied to the king, 'O Nebuchadnezzar, we do not need to defend ourselves before you in this matter. If we are thrown into the blazing furnace, the God we serve is able to save us from it, and he will rescue us from your hand, O king. But even if he does not, we want you to know, O king, that we will not serve your gods or worship the image of gold you have set up.'"

I love you!

Abba

_____

_____

_____

_____

_____

_____

_____

_____

_____

_____

_____

_____

_____

_____

_____

_____

_____

_____

_____

_____

_____

Day #173: _____ (date)

Let's begin our intimate conversation today with ...

Daniel 3:21, 24-26, "Then these men (Shadrach, Meshach, and Abed-Nego) were bound in their coats, their trousers, their turbans, and their other garments, and were cast into the midst of the burning fiery furnace. ...Then King Nebuchadnezzar was astonished; and he rose in haste and spoke, saying to his counselors, 'Did we not cast three men bound into the midst of the fire?' They answered and said to the king, 'True, O king.' 'Look!' he answered, 'I see four men loose, walking in the midst of the fire; and they are not hurt, and the form of the fourth is like the Son of God.' ... Then Shadrach, Meshach, and Abed-Nego came from the midst of the fire."

I love you!

Abba

_____

_____

_____

_____

_____

_____

_____

_____

_____

_____

_____

_____

_____

_____

_____

_____

_____

_____

_____

_____

_____

_____

Days #174 & #175: Rest and Reflect _____(dates)

Take some time to review what we shared over the past five days and record any new thoughts, feelings, insights, impressions, and responses. How did these intimate conversations impact you? How did they impact others as you interacted with them? What are you most grateful for?

I love you!

Abba

_____

_____

_____

_____

_____

_____

_____

_____

_____

_____

_____

_____

_____

_____

_____

_____

_____

_____

_____

_____

_____

_____

_____

_____

_____

_____

Day #176: _____ (date)

Let's begin our intimate conversation today with ...

Daniel 3:29, "'Therefore I (King Nebuchadnezzar) make a decree that any people, nation, or language which speaks anything amiss against the God of Shadrach, Meshach, and Abed-Nego shall be cut in pieces, and their houses shall be made an ash heap; because there is no other God who can deliver like this.'"

I love you!

Abba

_____

_____

_____

_____

_____

_____

_____

_____

_____

_____

_____

_____

_____

_____

_____

_____

_____

_____

_____

_____

_____

_____

_____

HOSEA: THEME- THE LOVE, FORGIVENESS AND RESTORATION OF GOD

In this book God chose the Prophet Hosea to illustrate the message of His unrelenting love and commitment to His unfaithful people. He instructed Hosea to marry Gomer, a prostitute. Gomer was unfaithful to Hosea several times. Even so, God told Hosea to seek her out, buy her back, and restore her to their marriage and family. This was a real life illustration of the kind of overwhelming love God has for sinners.

Day #177: _____ **(date)**

Let's begin our intimate conversation today with ...

Hosea 1:2-3 (NIV), "When the LORD began to speak through Hosea, the LORD said to him, 'Go, take to yourself an adulterous wife and children of unfaithfulness, because the land is guilty of the vilest adultery in departing from the LORD.' So he married Gomer daughter of Diblaim, and she conceived and bore him a son."

I love you!

Abba

_____

_____

_____

_____

_____

_____

_____

_____

_____

_____

_____

_____

_____

_____

_____

Day #178: _____ (date)

Let's begin our intimate conversation today with ...

Hosea 3:1-3 (NIV), "The LORD said to me, 'Go, show your love to your wife again, though she is loved by another and is an adulteress. Love her as the LORD loves the Israelites, though they turn to other gods and love the sacred raisin cakes.' So I bought her for fifteen shekels of silver and about a homer and a lethek of barley. Then I told her, 'You are to live with me many days; you must not be a prostitute or be intimate with any man, and I will live with you.'"

I love you!

Abba

_____

_____

_____

_____

_____

_____

_____

_____

_____

_____

_____

_____

_____

_____

_____

_____

_____

_____

_____

_____

_____

_____

Day #179: _____ **(date)**

Let's begin our intimate conversation today with ...

Hosea 6:6 (MSG), "I'm after love that lasts, not more religion. I want you to know GOD, not go to more prayer meetings."

I love you!

Abba

_____

_____

_____

_____

_____

_____

_____

_____

_____

_____

_____

_____

_____

_____

_____

_____

_____

_____

_____

_____

_____

_____

_____

_____

_____

Day #180: _____ **(date)**

Let's begin our intimate conversation today with ...

Hosea 14:9 (NIV), "Who is wise? He will realize these things. Who is discerning? He will understand them. The ways of the LORD are right; the righteous walk in them, but the rebellious stumble in them."

I love you!

Abba

_____

_____

_____

_____

_____

_____

_____

_____

_____

_____

_____

_____

_____

_____

_____

_____

_____

_____

_____

_____

_____

_____

_____

Day #181 & #182: Rest and Reflect _____(dates)

Take some time to review what we shared over the past five days and record any new thoughts, feelings, insights, impressions, and responses. How did these intimate conversations impact you? How did they impact others as you interacted with them? What are you most grateful for?

I love you!

Abba

_____

_____

_____

_____

_____

_____

_____

_____

_____

_____

_____

_____

_____

_____

_____

_____

_____

_____

_____

_____

_____

_____

_____

_____

JOEL: THEME- GOD'S JUDGMENT, GRACE AND RESTORATION

Joel's message is one of warning to the Israelites who had returned from exile. Woven into his message of God's judgment, and the need for repentance, is an affirmation of God's kindness and the blessings He promises to all who trust and follow Him.

Joel also foretold about the coming Messiah and the inauguration of the church age---a time when all people would be given the opportunity to call on the name of the Lord, be saved from their sins, and become participants in the kingdom of God.

Day #183: _____ (date)

Let's begin our intimate conversation today with ...

Joel 3:16-17, "The LORD also will roar from Zion, And utter His voice from Jerusalem; The heavens and earth will shake; But the LORD will be a shelter for His people, And the strength of the children of Israel. So you shall know that I am the LORD your God, Dwelling in Zion My holy mountain. Then Jerusalem shall be holy, And no aliens shall ever pass through her again."

I love you!

Abba

_____

_____

_____

_____

_____

_____

_____

_____

_____

_____

_____

_____

_____

_____

AMOS: THEME- JUDGMENT

God instructed the Prophet Amos, a shepherd, to share a very tough message with the people of Samaria, the capital of Israel. Idolatry was rampant and the people had become indifferent to God. The stern message was very similar to that of most of the prophets: God is slow to anger and willing to forgive. However, continued sin will bring judgment.

In the latter part of the final chapter Amos promises God's restoration for Israel.

Day #184: _____ (date)

Let's begin our intimate conversation today with ...

Amos 8:11-12 (NIV), "'The days are coming,' declares the Sovereign LORD, 'when I will send a famine through the land—not a famine of food or a thirst for water, but a famine of hearing the words of the LORD. Men will stagger from sea to sea and wander from north to east, searching for the word of the LORD, but they will not find it.'"

I love you!

Abba

_____

_____

_____

_____

_____

_____

_____

_____

_____

_____

_____

_____

_____

_____

_____

_____

Day #185: _____ (date)

Let's begin our intimate conversation today with ...

Amos 9:14-15 (NIV), "'I will bring back my exiled people Israel; they will rebuild the ruined cities and live in them. They will plant vineyards and drink their wine; they will make gardens and eat their fruit. I will plant Israel in their own land, never again to be uprooted from the land I have given them,' says the LORD your God."

I love you!

Abba

_____

_____

_____

_____

_____

_____

_____

_____

_____

_____

_____

_____

_____

_____

_____

_____

_____

_____

_____

_____

_____

_____

OBADIAH: THEME– GOD'S JUDGMENT ON EDOM

Obadiah, the shortest book in the Old Testament, is a dramatic example of God's response to anyone who would harm His children. Obadiah's assignment from God was to proclaim His judgment against the Edomites, whose indifference and arrogance toward Him, and their pride and treachery toward their relatives in Judah, would cause their destruction.

As Obadiah proclaimed the judgment to Edom, he assured the people of God that they would experience blessings and restoration to their land.

Day #186: _____ (date)

Let's begin our intimate conversation today with ...

Obadiah 1:3-4, "'The pride of your heart has deceived you, You who dwell in the clefts of the rock, Whose habitation is high; You who say in your heart, 'Who will bring me down to the ground?' Though you ascend as high as the eagle, And though you set your nest among the stars, From there I will bring you down,' says the LORD."

I love you!

Abba

_____

_____

_____

_____

_____

_____

_____

_____

_____

_____

_____

_____

_____

_____

Day #187: _____ **(date)**

Let's begin our intimate conversation today with ...

Obadiah 1:21 (NIV), "Deliverers will go up on Mount Zion to govern the mountains of Esau. And the kingdom will be the LORD's."

I love you!

Abba

_____

_____

_____

_____

_____

_____

_____

_____

_____

_____

_____

_____

_____

_____

_____

_____

_____

_____

_____

_____

_____

_____

_____

_____

Days #188 & #189: Rest and Reflect _____ (dates)

Take some time to review what we shared over the past five days and record any new thoughts, feelings, insights, impressions, and responses. How did these intimate conversations impact you? How did they impact others as you interacted with them? What are you most grateful for?

I love you!

Abba

_____

_____

_____

_____

_____

_____

_____

_____

_____

_____

_____

_____

_____

_____

_____

_____

_____

_____

_____

_____

_____

_____

JONAH: THEME- GOD'S GRACE TO ALL PEOPLE

God commissioned the Prophet Jonah to go to Nineveh, the capital of Assyria, to warn the people of impending destruction because of their wicked ways. Assyria was Israel's most dreaded enemy. Jonah wanted God to destroy them---not forgive them. Therefore, instead of following God's instructions, Jonah got on a ship headed in the opposite direction. The book of Jonah tells the story about Jonah's flight and how God stopped him and turned him around in the stomach of a giant fish. Jonah's story is a profound illustration of God's mercy and grace.

Day #190: _____ (date)

Let's begin our intimate conversation today with …

Jonah 1:1-3a, "Now the word of the LORD came to Jonah the son of Amittai, saying, 'Arise, go to Nineveh, that great city, and cry out against it; for their wickedness has come up before Me.' But Jonah arose to flee to Tarshish from the presence of the LORD."

I love you!

Abba

_____

_____

_____

_____

_____

_____

_____

_____

_____

_____

_____

_____

_____

Day #191: _____ (date)

Let's begin our intimate conversation today with ...

Jonah 3:10, "Then God saw their works, that they turned from their evil way; and God relented from the disaster that He had said He would bring upon them, and He did not do it."

I love you!

Abba

_____

_____

_____

_____

_____

_____

_____

_____

_____

_____

_____

_____

_____

_____

_____

_____

_____

_____

_____

_____

_____

_____

_____

Day #192: _____ (date)

Let's begin our intimate conversation today with ...

Jonah 4:1-2 (MSG), "Jonah was furious. He lost his temper. He yelled at GOD, 'GOD! I knew it—when I was back home, I knew this was going to happen! That's why I ran off to Tarshish! I knew you were sheer grace and mercy, not easily angered, rich in love, and ready at the drop of a hat to turn your plans of punishment into a program of forgiveness!'"

I love you!

Abba

_____

_____

_____

_____

_____

_____

_____

_____

_____

_____

_____

_____

_____

_____

_____

_____

_____

_____

_____

_____

_____

_____

MICAH: THEME– DIVINE JUDGMENT

The Prophet Micah condemns the rulers, priests, and prophets of Israel because they are misleading and exploiting the people. In Micah's day the people were very materially prosperous but devoid of integrity. Israel was bound to fall unless the nation turned back to God in wholehearted repentance. In this book Micah emphasizes God's pardoning of sin, compassion, and covenant faithfulness for His people. A prophecy about the coming of their Savior comes within a shepherding scene in Micah 2:12-13.

Day #193: _____ (date)

Let's begin our intimate conversation today with ...

Micah 2:12-13 (MSG), "'I'm calling a meeting, Jacob. I want everyone back—all the survivors of Israel. I'll get them together in one place—like sheep in a fold, like cattle in a corral—a milling throng of homebound people! Then I, GOD, will burst all confinements and lead them out into the open. They'll follow their King. I will be out in front leading them.'"

I love you!

Abba

_____

_____

_____

_____

_____

_____

_____

_____

_____

_____

_____

_____

_____

_____

_____

Day #194: _____ **(date)**

Let's begin our intimate conversation today with ...

Micah 6:8 (NIV), "He has showed you, O man, what is good. And what does the LORD require of you? To act justly and to love mercy and to walk humbly with your God."

I love you!

Abba

_____

_____

_____

_____

_____

_____

_____

_____

_____

_____

_____

_____

_____

_____

_____

_____

_____

_____

_____

_____

_____

_____

Days #195 and #196: Rest and Reflect _____ (dates)

Take some time to review what we shared over the past five days and record any new thoughts, feelings, insights, impressions, and responses. How did these intimate conversations impact you? How did they impact others as you interacted with them? What are you most grateful for?

I love you!

Abba

_____

_____

_____

_____

_____

_____

_____

_____

_____

_____

_____

_____

_____

_____

_____

_____

_____

_____

_____

_____

_____

_____

_____

Day #197: _____ (date)

Let's begin our intimate conversation today with ...

Micah 7:18-20 (MSG), "Where is the god who can compare to you—wiping the slate clean of guilt, Turning a blind eye, a deaf ear, to the past sins of your purged and precious people? You don't nurse your anger and don't stay angry long, for mercy is your specialty. That's what you love most. And compassion is on its way to us. You'll stamp out our wrongdoing. You'll sink our sins to the bottom of the ocean. You'll stay true to your word to Father Jacob and continue the compassion you showed Grandfather Abraham—Everything you promised our ancestors from a long time ago."

I love you!

Abba

_____

_____

_____

_____

_____

_____

_____

_____

_____

_____

_____

_____

_____

_____

_____

_____

_____

_____

_____

NAHUM: THEME– CONSOLATION

In this book God's great power is seen in the form of protection for the righteous as well as judgment for those rebelling against God and His ways. One hundred years after the Assyrians responded to Jonah's message of God's judgment with repentance, they returned to their evil ways. While God's judgment of Assyria is a theme of Nahum, the book is primarily a message of encouragement and comfort to His people in Judah, the southern kingdom of Israel.

Day #198: _____ (date)

Let's begin our intimate conversation today with ...

Nahum 1:7 (NIV), "The LORD is good, a refuge in times of trouble. He cares for those who trust in him."

I love you!

Abba

_____

_____

_____

_____

_____

_____

_____

_____

_____

_____

_____

_____

_____

_____

_____

_____

HABAKKUK: THEME— TRUSTING A SOVEREIGN GOD

This book tells Habakkuk's story of spiritual transformation. He begins his journey overwhelmed by circumstances and wondering why God's chosen people are suffering in their captivity. He senses that God is not with them and that the evil people are in control. At the end of the book Habakkuk has changed his focus from what he sees in the natural to placing his hope and trust in God. God's transformation of Habakkuk has taken him from doubt to trust and from complaining to joyful confidence as he realizes that God is sufficient in the midst of the challenging circumstances.

Day #199: _____ (date)

Let's begin our intimate conversation today with ...

Habakkuk 1:2 (NIV), "How long, O LORD, must I call for help, but you do not listen? Or cry out to you, 'Violence!' but you do not save?"

I love you!

Abba

_____

_____

_____

_____

_____

_____

_____

_____

_____

_____

_____

_____

_____

_____

_____

_____

Day #200: _____ (date)

Let's begin our intimate conversation today with ...

Habakkuk 2:4b (NIV), "'... but the righteous will live by his faith.'"

I love you!

Abba

_____

_____

_____

_____

_____

_____

_____

_____

_____

_____

_____

_____

_____

_____

_____

_____

_____

_____

_____

_____

_____

_____

_____

_____

_____

_____

Day #201: _____ (date)

Let's begin our intimate conversation today with ...

Habakkuk 3:17-19 (NIV), "Though the fig tree does not bud and there are no grapes on the vines, though the olive crop fails and the fields produce no food, though there are no sheep in the pen and no cattle in the stalls, yet I will rejoice in the LORD, I will be joyful in God my Savior. The Sovereign LORD is my strength; he makes my feet like the feet of a deer, he enables me to go on the heights."

I love you!

Abba

_____

_____

_____

_____

_____

_____

_____

_____

_____

_____

_____

_____

_____

_____

_____

_____

_____

_____

_____

_____

_____

_____

_____

Days #202 & #203: Rest and Reflect _____ **(dates)**

Take some time to review what we shared over the past five days and record any new thoughts, feelings, insights, impressions, and responses. How did these intimate conversations impact you? How did they impact others as you interacted with them? What are you most grateful for?

I love you!

Abba

_____

_____

_____

_____

_____

_____

_____

_____

_____

_____

_____

_____

_____

_____

_____

_____

_____

_____

_____

_____

_____

_____

_____

_____

ZEPHANIAH: THEME- THE WRATH OF A LOVING GOD

Few biblical writers describe the wrath of God or the joy of God as vividly as Zephaniah. The timeless message conveyed in this book is that God is both perfect justice and perfect love.

Day #204: _____ (date)

Let's begin our intimate conversation today with ...

Zephaniah 1:12, "And it shall come to pass at that time That I will search Jerusalem with lamps, And punish the men Who are settled in complacency, Who say in their heart, 'The LORD will not do good, Nor will He do evil.'"

I love you!

Abba

_____

_____

_____

_____

_____

_____

_____

_____

_____

_____

_____

_____

_____

_____

_____

_____

_____

_____

_____

Day #205: _____ (date)

Let's begin our intimate conversation today with ...

Zephaniah 1:14-15, 18a, "The great day of the LORD is near; It is near and
hastens quickly. The noise of the day of the LORD is bitter; There the mighty
men shall cry out. That day is a day of wrath, A day of trouble and distress, A day
of devastation and desolation, A day of darkness and gloominess, A day of clouds
and thick darkness, A day of trumpet and alarm Against the fortified cities And
against the high towers. ... Neither their silver nor their gold Shall be able to
deliver them In the day of the LORD's wrath."

I love you!

Abba

_____

_____

_____

_____

_____

_____

_____

_____

_____

_____

_____

_____

_____

_____

_____

_____

_____

_____

_____

_____

_____

_____

_____

Day #206: _____ (date)

Let's begin our intimate conversation today with ...

Zephaniah 3:14-15, 17 (NIV), "Sing, O Daughter of Zion; shout aloud, O Israel! Be glad and rejoice with all your heart, O Daughter of Jerusalem! The LORD has taken away your punishment, he has turned back your enemy. The LORD, the King of Israel, is with you; never again will you fear any harm. ... The LORD your God is with you, he is mighty to save. He will take great delight in you, he will quiet you with his love, he will rejoice over you with singing."

I love you!

Abba

_____
_____
_____
_____
_____
_____
_____
_____
_____
_____
_____
_____
_____
_____
_____
_____
_____
_____
_____
_____
_____

HAGGAI: THEME— REBUILDING THE TEMPLE

Haggai challenged the people to reconsider their priorities. They had become more focused on their own interests than their devotion to God. He encouraged them to glorify God by rebuilding the Temple in spite of many years of opposition and discouragement. The people responded by taking action. As they did this, there was a shift in their spiritual lives from devotion to self to devotion to God. This shift caused them to begin believing God for future blessings.

Day #207: _____ (date)

Let's begin our intimate conversation today with ...

Haggai 1:7-8 (NIV), "This is what the LORD Almighty says: 'Give careful thought to your ways. Go up into the mountains and bring down timber and build the house, so that I may take pleasure in it and be honored,' says the LORD."

I love you!

Abba

_____

_____

_____

_____

_____

_____

_____

_____

_____

_____

_____

_____

_____

_____

Day #208: _____ (date)

Let's begin our intimate conversation today with ...

Haggai 2:18-19 (MSG), "'Now think ahead from this same date—this twenty-fourth day of the ninth month. Think ahead from when the Temple rebuilding was launched. Has anything in your fields—vine, fig tree, pomegranate, olive tree—failed to flourish? From now on you can count on a blessing.'"

I love you!

Abba

_____

_____

_____

_____

_____

_____

_____

_____

_____

_____

_____

_____

_____

_____

_____

_____

_____

_____

_____

_____

_____

_____

_____

_____

Days #209 & #210: Rest and Reflect _____ (dates)

Take some time to review what we shared over the past five days and record any new thoughts, feelings, insights, impressions, and responses. How did these intimate conversations impact you? How did they impact others as you interacted with them? What are you most grateful for?

I love you!

Abba

_____

_____

_____

_____

_____

_____

_____

_____

_____

_____

_____

_____

_____

_____

_____

_____

_____

_____

_____

_____

_____

_____

_____

_____

ZECHARIAH: THEME- THE LORD REMEMBERS

God's people started out with great enthusiasm when they began to rebuild the Temple but discouragement and apathy set in when they experienced opposition. The Prophet Zechariah passionately continued Haggai's encouragement for them to restore the ruined Temple. He also shared eight visions with them, which assured His people of God's love and care.

Day #211: _____ **(date)**

Let's begin our intimate conversation today with ...

Zechariah 1:3, "... Thus says the LORD of hosts: 'Return to Me,' says the LORD of hosts, 'and I will return to you,' says the LORD of hosts."

I love you!

Abba

_____

_____

_____

_____

_____

_____

_____

_____

_____

_____

_____

_____

_____

_____

_____

_____

_____

_____

Day #212: _____ (date)

Let's begin our intimate conversation today with ...

Zechariah 9:9, "Rejoice greatly, O daughter of Zion! Shout, O daughter of
Jerusalem! Behold, your King is coming to you; He is just and having salvation,
Lowly and riding on a donkey, A colt, the foal of a donkey."

I love you!

Abba

_____

_____

_____

_____

_____

_____

_____

_____

_____

_____

_____

_____

_____

_____

_____

_____

_____

_____

_____

_____

_____

_____

_____

Day #213: _____ (date)

Let's begin our intimate conversation today with ...

Zechariah 14:8-9a, "And in that day it shall be That living waters shall flow from Jerusalem, Half of them toward the eastern sea And half of them toward the western sea; In both summer and winter it shall occur. And the LORD shall be King over all the earth."

I love you!

Abba

_____

_____

_____

_____

_____

_____

_____

_____

_____

_____

_____

_____

_____

_____

_____

_____

_____

_____

_____

_____

_____

_____

_____

MALACHI: THEME— REASSURANCE OF GOD'S LOVE AND JUSTICE

This is the last book in the Old Testament. Malachi was greatly burdened with the spiritual problems of his people and fervently addressed their disregard for the Lord.

Malachi also emphasized God's unchanging love for His people because of His mercy that endures forever.

Day #214: _____ **(date)**

Let's begin our intimate conversation today with ...

Malachi 3:6a, "For I am the LORD, I do not change:"

I love you!

Abba

_____

_____

_____

_____

_____

_____

_____

_____

_____

_____

_____

_____

_____

_____

_____

_____

_____

Day #215: _____ (date)

Let's begin our intimate conversation today with ...

Malachi 4:1-3, "'For behold, the day is coming, Burning like an oven, And all the proud, yes, all who do wickedly will be stubble. And the day which is coming shall burn them up,' Says the LORD of hosts, 'That will leave them neither root nor branch. But to you who fear My name The Sun of Righteousness shall arise With healing in His wings; And you shall go out And grow fat like stall-fed calves. You shall trample the wicked, For they shall be ashes under the soles of your feet On the day that I do this,' Says the LORD of hosts."

I love you!

Abba

_____
_____
_____
_____
_____
_____
_____
_____
_____
_____
_____
_____
_____
_____
_____
_____
_____
_____
_____

Days #216 & #217: Rest and Reflect _____(dates)

Take some time to review what we shared over the past five days and record any new thoughts, feelings, insights, impressions, and responses. How did these intimate conversations impact you? How did they impact others as you interacted with them? What are you most grateful for?

I love you!

Abba

_____

_____

_____

_____

_____

_____

_____

_____

_____

_____

_____

_____

_____

_____

_____

_____

_____

_____

_____

_____

_____

_____

_____

_____

_____

MATTHEW: THEME— JESUS CHRIST, THE MESSIAH, IS BORN

Matthew presents Jesus as both the long-awaited Messiah and the Son of David. His biography links the Old and New Testaments by showing how Christ fulfilled Old Testament prophecies about Him. This book also shows how the Law is filled with new meaning in the Person, words, and works of Jesus: Immanuel---God-With-Us.

Day #218: _____ (date)

Let's begin our intimate conversation today with ...

Matthew 1:23, "'Behold, the virgin shall be with child, and bear a Son, and they shall call His name Immanuel,' which is translated, 'God with us.'"

I love you!

Abba

_____

_____

_____

_____

_____

_____

_____

_____

_____

_____

_____

_____

_____

_____

_____

_____

_____

_____

Day #219: _____ **(date)**

Let's begin our intimate conversation today with ...

Matthew 3:1-2, "In those days John the Baptist came preaching in the wilderness of Judea, and saying, 'Repent, for the kingdom of heaven is at hand!'"

I love you!

Abba

_____

_____

_____

_____

_____

_____

_____

_____

_____

_____

_____

_____

_____

_____

_____

_____

_____

_____

_____

_____

_____

_____

Day #220: _____ (date)

Let's begin our intimate conversation today with ...

Matthew 4:18-20, "And Jesus, walking by the Sea of Galilee, saw two brothers, Simon called Peter, and Andrew his brother, casting a net into the sea; for they were fishermen. Then He said to them, 'Follow Me, and I will make you fishers of men.' They immediately left their nets and followed Him."

I love you!

Abba

_____

_____

_____

_____

_____

_____

_____

_____

_____

_____

_____

_____

_____

_____

_____

_____

_____

_____

_____

_____

_____

_____

_____

_____

Day #221: _____ (date)

Let's begin our intimate conversation today with ...

Matthew 5:3 (MSG), Jesus speaking: "You're blessed when you're at the end of your rope. With less of you there is more of God and his rule."

I love you!

Abba

_____

_____

_____

_____

_____

_____

_____

_____

_____

_____

_____

_____

_____

_____

_____

_____

_____

_____

_____

_____

_____

_____

_____

_____

_____

Day #222: _____ (date)

Let's begin our intimate conversation today with ...

Matthew 5:16, Jesus speaking: "Let your light so shine before men, that they may see your good works and glorify your Father in heaven."

I love you!

Abba

_____

_____

_____

_____

_____

_____

_____

_____

_____

_____

_____

_____

_____

_____

_____

_____

_____

_____

_____

_____

_____

_____

Days #223 & #224: Rest and Reflect _____ **(dates)**

Take some time to review what we shared over the past five days and record any new thoughts, feelings, insights, impressions, and responses. How did these intimate conversations impact you? How did they impact others as you interacted with them? What are you most grateful for?

I love you!

Abba

_____

_____

_____

_____

_____

_____

_____

_____

_____

_____

_____

_____

_____

_____

_____

_____

_____

_____

_____

_____

_____

_____

Day #225: _____ **(date)**

Let's begin our intimate conversation today with ...

Matthew 6:9-10 (NIV), Jesus speaking: "This, then, is how you should pray: 'Our Father in heaven, hallowed be your name, your kingdom come, your will be done on earth as it is in heaven.'"

I love you!

Abba

_____

_____

_____

_____

_____

_____

_____

_____

_____

_____

_____

_____

_____

_____

_____

_____

_____

_____

_____

_____

_____

_____

_____

_____

_____

_____

Day #226: _____ (date)

Let's begin our intimate conversation today with ...

Matthew 6:24, Jesus speaking: "No one can serve two masters; for either he will hate the one and love the other, or else he will be loyal to the one and despise the other. You cannot serve God and mammon."

I love you!

Abba

_____

_____

_____

_____

_____

_____

_____

_____

_____

_____

_____

_____

_____

_____

_____

_____

_____

_____

_____

_____

_____

_____

_____

_____

_____

_____

Day #227: _____ (date)

Let's begin our intimate conversation today with ...

Matthew 11:28, Jesus speaking: "Come to Me, all you who labor and are heavy laden, and I will give you rest."

I love you!

Abba

_____

_____

_____

_____

_____

_____

_____

_____

_____

_____

_____

_____

_____

_____

_____

_____

_____

_____

_____

_____

_____

_____

_____

_____

_____

_____

_____

Day #228: _____ (date)

Let's begin our intimate conversation today with ...

Matthew 22:36-40, "'Teacher, which is the greatest commandment in the law?' Jesus said to him, 'You shall love the LORD your God with all your heart, with all your soul, and with all your mind. This is the first and great commandment. And the second is like it: You shall love your neighbor as yourself. On these two commandments hang all the Law and the Prophets.'"

I love you!

Abba

_____

_____

_____

_____

_____

_____

_____

_____

_____

_____

_____

_____

_____

_____

_____

_____

_____

_____

_____

_____

_____

_____

Day #229: _____ (date)

Let's begin our intimate conversation today with ...

Matthew 28:18-20 (NIV), "Then Jesus came to them and said, 'All authority in heaven and on earth has been given to me. Therefore go and make disciples of all nations, baptizing them in the name of the Father and of the Son and of the Holy Spirit, and teaching them to obey everything I have commanded you. And surely I am with you always, to the very end of the age.'"

I love you!

Abba

_____

_____

_____

_____

_____

_____

_____

_____

_____

_____

_____

_____

_____

_____

_____

_____

_____

_____

_____

_____

_____

_____

Days #230 & #231: Rest and Reflect _____ **(dates)**

Take some time to review what we shared over the past five days and record any new thoughts, feelings, insights, impressions, and responses. How did these intimate conversations impact you? How did they impact others as you interacted with them? What are you most grateful for?

I love you!

Abba

_____

_____

_____

_____

_____

_____

_____

_____

_____

_____

_____

_____

_____

_____

_____

_____

_____

_____

_____

_____

_____

_____

MARK: THEME- JESUS, THE SUFFERING SERVANT, CAME TO SAVE

Mark wrote this book to encourage the early Christians by presenting Jesus as the Servant-Messiah. Jesus' entire ministry is set within the context of the self-giving love of the Son of God, climaxed in the Cross and Resurrection.

Day #232: _____ **(date)**

Let's begin our intimate conversation today with ...

Mark 1:35 (NIV), "Very early in the morning, while it was still dark, Jesus got up, left the house and went off to a solitary place, where he prayed."

I love you!

Abba

_____

_____

_____

_____

_____

_____

_____

_____

_____

_____

_____

_____

_____

_____

_____

_____

_____

_____

_____

_____

Day #233: _____ (date)

Let's begin our intimate conversation today with ...

Mark 1:40-42, "Now a leper came to Him, imploring Him, kneeling down to Him and saying to Him, 'If You are willing, You can make me clean.' Then Jesus, moved with compassion, stretched out His hand and touched him, and said to him, 'I am willing; be cleansed.' As soon as He had spoken, immediately the leprosy left him, and he was cleansed."

I love you!

Abba

_____

_____

_____

_____

_____

_____

_____

_____

_____

_____

_____

_____

_____

_____

_____

_____

_____

_____

_____

_____

_____

Day #234: _____ (date)

Let's begin our intimate conversation today with ...

Mark 4:37-41, "And a great windstorm arose, and the waves beat into the boat, so that it was already filling. But He (Jesus) was in the stern, asleep on a pillow. And they awoke Him and said to Him, 'Teacher, do You not care that we are perishing?' Then He arose and rebuked the wind, and said to the sea, 'Peace, be still!' And the wind ceased and there was a great calm. But He said to them, 'Why are you so fearful? How is it that you have no faith?' And they feared exceedingly, and said to one another, 'Who can this be, that even the wind and the sea obey Him!'"

I love you!

Abba

_____

_____

_____

_____

_____

_____

_____

_____

_____

_____

_____

_____

_____

_____

_____

_____

_____

_____

_____

_____

_____

Day #235: _____ (date)

Let's begin our intimate conversation today with ...

Mark 10:17, 20-23 (MSG), "As he (Jesus) went out into the street, a man came running up, greeted him with great reverence, and asked, 'Good Teacher, what must I do to get eternal life?' ... He said, 'Teacher, I have—from my youth—kept them all (10 Commandments)!' Jesus looked him hard in the eye—and loved him! He said, 'There's one thing left: Go sell whatever you own and give it to the poor. All your wealth will then be heavenly wealth. And come follow me.' The man's face clouded over. This was the last thing he expected to hear, and he walked off with a heavy heart. He was holding on tight to a lot of things, and not about to let go. Looking at his disciples, Jesus said, 'Do you have any idea how difficult it is for people who 'have it all' to enter God's kingdom?'"

I love you!

Abba

_____

_____

_____

_____

_____

_____

_____

_____

_____

_____

_____

_____

_____

_____

_____

_____

_____

_____

_____

Day #236: _____ **(date)**

Let's begin our intimate conversation today with ...

Mark 10:45, "For even the Son of Man did not come to be served, but to serve, and to give His life a ransom for many."

I love you!

Abba

_____

_____

_____

_____

_____

_____

_____

_____

_____

_____

_____

_____

_____

_____

_____

_____

_____

_____

_____

_____

_____

_____

_____

Days #237 & #238: Rest and Reflect _____(dates)

Take some time to review what we shared over the past five days and record any new thoughts, feelings, insights, impressions, and responses. How did these intimate conversations impact you? How did they impact others as you interacted with them? What are you most grateful for?

I love you!

Abba

_____

_____

_____

_____

_____

_____

_____

_____

_____

_____

_____

_____

_____

_____

_____

_____

_____

_____

_____

_____

_____

_____

_____

LUKE: THEME- JESUS, THE SAVIOR OF THE WORLD

Luke never met Jesus but was an excellent researcher and historian. This book is the longest Gospel, giving the fullest portrayal of Jesus' life and ministry. A unique feature of Luke's Gospel is its focus on Jesus not only being the Jewish Deliverer, but the Savior of the entire world.

Day #239: _____ **(date)**

Let's begin our intimate conversation today with ...

Satan tempts Jesus three times:

Luke 4:3-9, 12-13, "And the devil said to Him, 'If You are the Son of God, command this stone to become bread.' But Jesus answered him, saying, 'It is written, Man shall not live by bread alone, but by every word of God.' Then the devil, taking Him up on a high mountain, showed Him all the kingdoms of the world in a moment of time. And the devil said to Him, 'All this authority I will give to You, and their glory; for this has been delivered to me, and I give it to whomever I wish. Therefore, if You will worship before me, all will be Yours.' And Jesus answered and said to him, 'Get behind Me, Satan! For it is written, You shall worship the LORD your God, and Him only you shall serve.' Then he brought Him to Jerusalem, set Him on the pinnacle of the temple, and said to Him, 'If You are the Son of God, throw Yourself down from here.' ... And Jesus answered and said to him, 'It has been said, You shall not tempt the LORD your God.' Now when the devil had ended every temptation, he departed from Him until an opportune time."

I love you!

Abba

_____

_____

_____

_____

_____

_____

_____

_____

Day #240: _____ **(date)**

Let's begin our intimate conversation today with ...

Luke 4:18-19, Jesus speaking: "The Spirit of the LORD is upon Me, Because He has anointed Me To preach the gospel to the poor; He has sent Me to heal the brokenhearted, To proclaim liberty to the captives And recovery of sight to the blind, To set at liberty those who are oppressed; To proclaim the acceptable year of the LORD."

I love you!

Abba

_____

_____

_____

_____

_____

_____

_____

_____

_____

_____

_____

_____

_____

_____

_____

_____

_____

_____

_____

Day #241: _____ **(date)**

Let's begin our intimate conversation today with ...

Luke 6:43-44a (NIV), "No good tree bears bad fruit, nor does a bad tree bear good fruit. Each tree is recognized by its own fruit."

I love you!

Abba

_____

_____

_____

_____

_____

_____

_____

_____

_____

_____

_____

_____

_____

_____

_____

_____

_____

_____

_____

_____

_____

_____

_____

_____

Day #242: _____ (date)

Let's begin our intimate conversation today with ...

Luke 9:23-24 (MSG), "Then he (Jesus) told them what they could expect for themselves: 'Anyone who intends to come with me has to let me lead. You're not in the driver's seat—I am. Don't run from suffering; embrace it. Follow me and I'll show you how. Self-help is no help at all. Self-sacrifice is the way, my way, to finding yourself, your true self.'"

I love you!

Abba

_____

_____

_____

_____

_____

_____

_____

_____

_____

_____

_____

_____

_____

_____

_____

_____

_____

_____

_____

_____

_____

Day #243: _____ (date)

Let's begin our intimate conversation today with ...

Luke 19:10 (NIV), Jesus speaking: "For the Son of Man came to seek and to save what was lost."

I love you!

Abba

_____

_____

_____

_____

_____

_____

_____

_____

_____

_____

_____

_____

_____

_____

_____

_____

_____

_____

_____

_____

_____

_____

_____

_____

Days #244 & #245: Rest and Reflect _____(dates)

Take some time to review what we shared over the past five days and record any new thoughts, feelings, insights, impressions, and responses. How did these intimate conversations impact you? How did they impact others as you interacted with them? What are you most grateful for?

I love you!

Abba

_____

_____

_____

_____

_____

_____

_____

_____

_____

_____

_____

_____

_____

_____

_____

_____

_____

_____

_____

_____

_____

_____

_____

JOHN: THEME- KNOWING GOD BY BELIEVING IN JESUS

John wrote his eyewitness account of the life, death, and resurrection of Jesus Christ for the purpose of proclaiming Him to be the promised Messiah. He also emphasized that the only way to live eternally with God was to trust Jesus for salvation.

In this book John shows Jesus declaring His identity through seven "I am" statements: "bread of life"- "light of the world"- "gate for the sheep"- "good shepherd"- "resurrection and the life"- "the way, and the truth, and the life"- and the "true vine".

Day #246: _____ (date)

Let's begin our intimate conversation today with ...

John 1:1, 14, "In the beginning was the Word, and the Word was with God, and the Word was God. ...And the Word became flesh and dwelt among us, and we beheld His glory, the glory as of the only begotten of the Father, full of grace and truth."

I love you!

Abba

_____

_____

_____

Day #247: _____ (date)

Let's begin our intimate conversation today with ...

John 3:16-17 (NIV), Jesus speaking: "For God so loved the world that he gave his one and only Son, that whoever believes in him shall not perish but have eternal life. For God did not send his Son into the world to condemn the world, but to save the world through him."

I love you!

Abba

_____

_____

_____

_____

_____

_____

_____

_____

_____

_____

_____

_____

_____

_____

_____

_____

_____

_____

_____

_____

_____

_____

_____

Day #248: _____ (date)

Let's begin our intimate conversation today with ...

John 10:10, Jesus speaking: "The thief does not come except to steal, and to kill, and to destroy. I have come that they may have life, and that they may have it more abundantly."

I love you!

Abba

_____

_____

_____

_____

_____

_____

_____

_____

_____

_____

_____

_____

_____

_____

_____

_____

_____

_____

_____

_____

_____

_____

_____

_____

_____

Day #249: _____ **(date)**

Let's begin our intimate conversation today with ...

John 14:6-7 (NIV), "Jesus answered, 'I am the way and the truth and the life. No one comes to the Father except through me. If you really knew me, you would know my Father as well. From now on, you do know him and have seen him.'"

I love you!

Abba

_____

_____

_____

_____

_____

_____

_____

_____

_____

_____

_____

_____

_____

_____

_____

_____

_____

_____

_____

_____

_____

_____

_____

Day #250: _____ (date)

Let's begin our intimate conversation today with ...

John 15:9, Jesus speaking: "As the Father loved Me, I also have loved you; abide in My love."

I love you!

Abba

_____

_____

_____

_____

_____

_____

_____

_____

_____

_____

_____

_____

_____

_____

_____

_____

_____

_____

_____

_____

_____

_____

_____

_____

_____

Days #251 & #252: Rest and Reflect _____ **(dates)**

Take some time to review what we shared over the past five days and record any new thoughts, feelings, insights, impressions, and responses. How did these intimate conversations impact you? How did they impact others as you interacted with them? What are you most grateful for?

I love you!

Abba

_____

_____

_____

_____

_____

_____

_____

_____

_____

_____

_____

_____

_____

_____

_____

_____

_____

_____

_____

_____

_____

ACTS: THEME- THE SPREAD OF CHRISTIANITY

Acts is a book about transitions--from Judaism to Christianity, from law to grace. It records the promised outpouring of the Holy Spirit and subsequent spread of the gospel message from Jerusalem to Rome.

Day #253: _____ **(date)**

Let's begin our intimate conversation today with ...

Acts 1:8, Jesus speaking: "But you shall receive power when the Holy Spirit has come upon you; and you shall be witnesses to Me in Jerusalem, and in all Judea and Samaria, and to the end of the earth."

I love you!

Abba

_____

_____

_____

_____

_____

_____

_____

_____

_____

_____

_____

_____

_____

_____

_____

_____

_____

_____

Day #254: _____ (date)

Let's begin our intimate conversation today with ...

Acts 2:17, 21 (NIV), "In the last days, God says, I will pour out my Spirit on all people. Your sons and daughters will prophesy, your young men will see visions, your old men will dream dreams. ...And everyone who calls on the name of the Lord will be saved."

I love you!

Abba

_____

_____

_____

_____

_____

_____

_____

_____

_____

_____

_____

_____

_____

_____

_____

_____

_____

_____

_____

_____

_____

_____

_____

_____

Day #255: _____ (date)

Let's begin our intimate conversation today with ...

Acts 16:23-26 (Paul & Silas in prison-NIV), "After they had been severely flogged, they were thrown into prison, and the jailer was commanded to guard them carefully. Upon receiving such orders, he put them in the inner cell and fastened their feet in the stocks. About midnight Paul and Silas were praying and singing hymns to God, and the other prisoners were listening to them. Suddenly there was such a violent earthquake that the foundations of the prison were shaken. At once all the prison doors flew open, and everybody's chains came loose."

I love you!

Abba

_____

_____

_____

_____

_____

_____

_____

_____

_____

_____

_____

_____

_____

_____

_____

_____

_____

_____

_____

_____

_____

_____

_____

Day #256: _____ (date)

Let's begin our intimate conversation today with ...

Acts 26:15-18, Paul recounts his conversion experience: "So I said, 'Who are you Lord?' And He said, 'I am Jesus, whom you are persecuting. But rise and stand on your feet; for I have appeared to you for this purpose, to make you a minister and a witness both of the things which you have seen and of the things which I will yet reveal to you. I will deliver you from the Jewish people, as well as from the Gentiles, to whom I now send you, to open their eyes, in order to turn them from darkness to light, and from the power of Satan to God, that they may receive forgiveness of sins and an inheritance among those who are sanctified by faith in Me.'"

I love you!

Abba

_____

_____

_____

_____

_____

_____

_____

_____

_____

_____

_____

_____

_____

_____

_____

_____

_____

_____

_____

_____

ROMANS: THEME—THE RIGHTEOUSNESS OF GOD

Paul boldly proclaimed the liberating message of Jesus Christ because he personally knew its power to turn a life completely around. He wrote this letter to the early Christians in Rome. He explained to them that because of God's great love, grace, and mercy they are forgiven through faith in Christ and their response should be to live a life consistent with God's own righteousness.

Day #257: _____ **(date)**

Let's begin our intimate conversation today with ...

Romans 5:8 (NIV), "But God demonstrates his own love for us in this: While we were still sinners, Christ died for us."

I love you!

Abba

_____

_____

_____

_____

_____

_____

_____

_____

_____

_____

_____

_____

_____

_____

_____

_____

_____

Days #258 & #259: Rest and Reflect _____(dates)

Take some time to review what we shared over the past five days and record any new thoughts, feelings, insights, impressions, and responses. How did these intimate conversations impact you? How did they impact others as you interacted with them? What are you most grateful for?

I love you!

Abba

_____
_____
_____
_____
_____
_____
_____
_____
_____
_____
_____
_____
_____
_____
_____
_____
_____
_____
_____
_____
_____
_____
_____
_____

Day #260: _____ (date)

Let's begin our intimate conversation today with ...

Romans 8:1-2, "There is therefore now no condemnation to those who are in Christ Jesus, who do not walk according to the flesh, but according to the Spirit. For the law of the Spirit of life in Christ Jesus has made me free from the law of sin and death."

I love you!

Abba

_____

_____

_____

_____

_____

_____

_____

_____

_____

_____

_____

_____

_____

_____

_____

_____

_____

_____

_____

_____

_____

_____

_____

_____

Day #261: _____ **(date)**

Let's begin our intimate conversation today with ...

Romans 8:5-6 (NIV), "Those who live according to the sinful nature have their minds set on what that nature desires; but those who live in accordance with the Spirit have their minds set on what the Spirit desires. The mind of sinful man is death, but the mind controlled by the Spirit is life and peace."

I love you!

Abba

_____

_____

_____

_____

_____

_____

_____

_____

_____

_____

_____

_____

_____

_____

_____

_____

_____

_____

_____

_____

_____

_____

_____

Day #262: _____ **(date)**

Let's begin our intimate conversation today with ...

Romans 8:15-17 (NIV), "For you did not receive a spirit that makes you a slave
again to fear, but you received the Spirit of sonship. And by him we cry, 'Abba,
Father.' The Spirit himself testifies with our spirit that we are God's children.
Now if we are children, then we are heirs—heirs of God and co-heirs with Christ,
if indeed we share in his sufferings in order that we may also share in his glory."

I love you!

Abba

_____

_____

_____

_____

_____

_____

_____

_____

_____

_____

_____

_____

_____

_____

_____

_____

_____

_____

_____

_____

_____

_____

_____

Day #263: _____ (date)

Let's begin our intimate conversation today with ...

Romans 8:38-39 (MSG), "I'm absolutely convinced that nothing—nothing living or dead, angelic or demonic, today or tomorrow, high or low, thinkable or unthinkable—absolutely *nothing* can get between us and God's love because of the way that Jesus our Master has embraced us."

I love you!

Abba

_____
_____
_____
_____
_____
_____
_____
_____
_____
_____
_____
_____
_____
_____
_____
_____
_____
_____
_____
_____
_____

Day #264: _____ (date)

Let's begin our intimate conversation today with ...

Romans 12:1-2 (MSG), "So here's what I want you to do, God helping you: Take your everyday, ordinary life—your sleeping, eating, going-to-work, and walking-around life—and place it before God as an offering. Embracing what God does for you is the best thing you can do for him. Don't become so well-adjusted to your culture that you fit into it without even thinking. Instead, fix your attention on God. You'll be changed from the inside out. Readily recognize what he wants from you, and quickly respond to it. Unlike the culture around you, always dragging you down to its level of immaturity, God brings the best out of you, develops well-formed maturity in you."

I love you!

Abba

_____
_____
_____
_____
_____
_____
_____
_____
_____
_____
_____
_____
_____
_____
_____
_____
_____
_____
_____
_____
_____
_____

Days #265 & #266: Rest and Reflect _____(dates)

Take some time to review what we shared over the past five days and record
any new thoughts, feelings, insights, impressions, and responses. How did
these intimate conversations impact you? How did they impact others as you
interacted with them? What are you most grateful for?

I love you!

Abba

_____

_____

_____

_____

_____

_____

_____

_____

_____

_____

_____

_____

_____

_____

_____

_____

_____

_____

_____

_____

_____

_____

_____

I CORINTHIANS: THEME- CHRISTIAN CONDUCT

Corinth was the most important city of ancient Greece. It was known for its commercial prosperity and its immorality. In this book Paul challenged the young Christians at Corinth to be very careful not to blend in with the culture and accept its values and life-styles. He encouraged them to pursue holiness and live a Christ-centered life.

Day #267: _____ **(date)**

Let's begin our intimate conversation today with ...

1 Corinthians 10:12-13 (MSG), "Don't be so naïve and self-confident. You're not exempt. You could fall flat on your face as easily as anyone else. Forget about self-confidence; it's useless. Cultivate God-confidence. No test or temptation that comes your way is beyond the course of what others have had to face. All you need to remember is that God will never let you down; he'll never let you be pushed past your limit; he'll always be there to help you come through it."

I love you!

Abba

_____

_____

_____

_____

_____

_____

_____

_____

_____

_____

_____

_____

_____

_____

_____

Day #268: _____ (date)

Let's begin our intimate conversation today with ...

1 Corinthians 10:31-32a (NIV), "So whether you eat or drink or whatever you do, do it all for the glory of God. Do not cause anyone to stumble...."

I love you!

Abba

_____

_____

_____

_____

_____

_____

_____

_____

_____

_____

_____

_____

_____

_____

_____

_____

_____

_____

_____

_____

_____

_____

_____

_____

Day #269: _____ **(date)**

Let's begin our intimate conversation today with ...

1 Corinthians 12:25-27a (MSG), "The way God designed our bodies is a model for understanding our lives together as a church: every part dependent on every other part, the parts we mention and the parts we don't, the parts we see and the parts we don't. If one part hurts, every other part is involved in the hurt, and in the healing. If one part flourishes, every other part enters into the exuberance. You are Christ's body—that's who you are!"

I love you!

Abba

_____

_____

_____

_____

_____

_____

_____

_____

_____

_____

_____

_____

_____

_____

_____

_____

_____

_____

_____

_____

_____

_____

_____

_____

Day #270: _____ (date)

Let's begin our intimate conversation today with ...

1 Corinthians 13:4-8a (NIV), "Love is patient, love is kind. It does not envy, it does not boast, it is not proud. It is not rude, it is not self-seeking, it is not easily angered, it keeps no record of wrongs. Love does not delight in evil but rejoices with the truth. It always protects, always trusts, always hopes, always perseveres. Love never fails."

I love you!

Abba

_____

_____

_____

_____

_____

_____

_____

_____

_____

_____

_____

_____

_____

_____

_____

_____

_____

_____

_____

_____

_____

2 CORINTHIANS: THEME—POWERFUL MINISTRY THROUGH WEAK INDIVIDUALS

In this letter you see Paul defending himself against critics and false teachers who had infiltrated the church at Corinth. Yet, Paul shows his love to the loyal majority of Christians in Corinth, while also giving a rebuke to the ones who are rebelling. He emphasizes that the focus of all service to God needs to be Jesus.

Day #271: _____ **(date)**

Let's begin our intimate conversation today with ...

2 Corinthians 5:7 (NIV), "We live by faith, not by sight."

I love you!

Abba

_____

_____

_____

_____

_____

_____

_____

_____

_____

_____

_____

_____

_____

_____

_____

_____

_____

_____

_____

Days #272 & #273: Rest and Reflect _____ **(dates)**

Take some time to review what we shared over the past five days and record any new thoughts, feelings, insights, impressions, and responses. How did these intimate conversations impact you? How did they impact others as you interacted with them? What are you most grateful for?

I love you!

Abba

_____

_____

_____

_____

_____

_____

_____

_____

_____

_____

_____

_____

_____

_____

_____

_____

_____

_____

_____

_____

_____

_____

_____

_____

_____

_____

Day #274: _____ **(date)**

Let's begin our intimate conversation today with ...

2 Corinthians 5:17 (NIV), "Therefore, if anyone is in Christ, he is a new creation; the old has gone, the new has come!"

I love you!

Abba

_____

_____

_____

_____

_____

_____

_____

_____

_____

_____

_____

_____

_____

_____

_____

_____

_____

_____

_____

_____

_____

Day #275: _____ **(date)**

Let's begin our intimate conversation today with ...

2 Corinthians 10:3-5 (NIV), "For though we live in the world, we do not wage war as the world does. The weapons we fight with are not the weapons of the world. On the contrary, they have divine power to demolish strongholds. We demolish arguments and every pretension that sets itself up against the knowledge of God, and we take captive every thought to make it obedient to Christ."

I love you!

Abba

_____
_____
_____
_____
_____
_____
_____
_____
_____
_____
_____
_____
_____
_____
_____
_____
_____
_____

Day #276: _____ (date)

Let's begin our intimate conversation today with ...

2 Corinthians 12:9 (MSG), "...'My grace is enough; it's all you need. My strength comes into its own in your weakness.' Once I heard that, I was glad to let it happen. I quit focusing on the handicap and began appreciating the gift. It was a case of Christ's strength moving in on my weakness."

I love you!

Abba

_____

_____

_____

_____

_____

_____

_____

_____

_____

_____

_____

_____

_____

_____

_____

_____

_____

_____

_____

_____

_____

_____

_____

GALATIANS: THEME- FREEDOM IN CHRIST

Paul wrote this letter to explain that salvation was by grace through faith in Jesus alone. His goal was to counteract the confusion that was being caused by the teachings of the Judaizers. The Judaizers did not deny that faith in Jesus was necessary for salvation but insisted that just faith in Jesus was inadequate because they were still bound to follow the Jewish law in order to be accepted by God.

Day #277: _____ **(date)**

Let's begin our intimate conversation today with ...

Galatians 2:20-21 (NIV), "I have been crucified with Christ and I no longer live, but Christ lives in me. The life I live in the body, I live by faith in the Son of God, who loved me and gave himself for me. I do not set aside the grace of God, for if righteousness could be gained through the law, Christ died for nothing!"

I love you!

Abba

_____

_____

_____

_____

_____

_____

_____

_____

_____

_____

_____

_____

_____

_____

_____

_____

Day #278: _____ (date)

Let's begin our intimate conversation today with ...

Galatians 4:4-7 (MSG), "But when the time arrived that was set by God the Father, God sent his Son, born among us of a woman, born under the conditions of the law so that he might redeem those of us who have been kidnapped by the law. Thus we have been set free to experience our rightful heritage. You can tell for sure that you are now fully adopted as his own children because God sent the Spirit of his son into our lives crying out, 'Papa! Father!' Doesn't that privilege of intimate conversation with God make it plain that you are not a slave, but a child? And if you are a child, you're also an heir, with complete access to the inheritance."

I love you!

Abba

_____
_____
_____
_____
_____
_____
_____
_____
_____
_____
_____
_____
_____
_____
_____
_____
_____
_____
_____
_____

Days #279 & #280: Rest and Reflect _____(dates)

Take some time to review what we shared over the past five days and record any new thoughts, feelings, insights, impressions, and responses. How did these intimate conversations impact you? How did they impact others as you interacted with them? What are you most grateful for?

I love you!

Abba

_____

_____

_____

_____

_____

_____

_____

_____

_____

_____

_____

_____

_____

_____

_____

_____

_____

_____

_____

_____

_____

Day #281: _____ (date)

Let's begin our intimate conversation today with ...

Galatians 5:16, 22-23 (NIV), "So I say, live by the Spirit, and you will not gratify the desires of the sinful nature. ...But the fruit of the Spirit is love, joy, peace, patience, kindness, goodness, faithfulness, gentleness and self-control. Against such things there is no law."

I love you!

Abba

_____

_____

_____

_____

_____

_____

_____

_____

_____

_____

_____

_____

_____

_____

_____

_____

_____

_____

_____

_____

_____

_____

_____

_____

Day #282: _____ (date)

Let's begin our intimate conversation today with ...

Galatians 6:7-8, "Do not be deceived, God is not mocked; for whatever a man sows, that he will also reap."

I love you!

Abba

_____

_____

_____

_____

_____

_____

_____

_____

_____

_____

_____

_____

_____

_____

_____

_____

_____

_____

_____

_____

_____

_____

_____

_____

EPHESIANS: THEME— THE ROLE OF THE CHURCH IN GOD'S GLORIOUS PLAN

Paul wrote this letter to the Christians in Ephesus while he was a prisoner in Rome for preaching the gospel. In this letter Paul reveals God's intentions to form a body, the church, to express Christ's fullness on earth. His major purpose in this letter was to encourage, equip, and empower the maturing church.

Day #283: _____ **(date)**

Let's begin our intimate conversation today with ...

Ephesians 2:8-10, "For by grace you have been saved through faith, and that not of yourselves; it is the gift of God, not of works, lest anyone should boast. For we are His workmanship, created in Christ Jesus for good works, which God prepared beforehand that we should walk in them."

I love you!

Abba

_____

_____

_____

_____

_____

_____

_____

_____

_____

_____

_____

_____

_____

_____

_____

_____

Day #284: _____ (date)

Let's begin our intimate conversation today with ...

Ephesians 3:20-21 (MSG), "God can do anything, you know—far more than you could ever imagine or guess or request in your wildest dreams! He does it not by pushing us around but by working within us, his Spirit deeply and gently within us. Glory to God in the church! Glory to God in the Messiah, in Jesus! Glory down all the generations! Glory through all millennia! Oh, yes!"

I love you!

Abba

_____

_____

_____

_____

_____

_____

_____

_____

_____

_____

_____

_____

_____

_____

_____

_____

_____

_____

_____

_____

Day #285: _____ **(date)**

Let's begin our intimate conversation today with ...

Ephesians 4:21-24 (MSG), "My assumption is that you have paid careful attention to him (Jesus), been well instructed in the truth precisely as we have it in Jesus. Since, then, we do not have the excuse of ignorance, everything—and I do mean everything—connected with that old way of life has to go. It's rotten through and through. Get rid of it! And then take on an entirely new way of life—a God-fashioned life, a life renewed from the inside and working itself into your conduct as God accurately reproduces his character in you."

I love you!

Abba

Days #286 & #287: Rest and Reflect _____ (dates)

Take some time to review what we shared over the past five days and record any new thoughts, feelings, insights, impressions, and responses. How did these intimate conversations impact you? How did they impact others as you interacted with them? What are you most grateful for?

I love you!

Abba

_____

_____

_____

_____

_____

_____

_____

_____

_____

_____

_____

_____

_____

_____

_____

_____

_____

_____

_____

_____

_____

_____

Day #288: _____ **(date)**

Let's begin our intimate conversation today with ...

Ephesians 6:10-11 (NIV), "Finally, be strong in the Lord and in his mighty power. Put on the full armor of God so that you can take your stand against the devil's schemes. " (Armor: belt of truth, breastplate of righteousness, gospel of peace, shield of faith, helmet of salvation, and sword of the Spirit- verses 14-17)

I love you!

Abba

Read - Reflect - Respond - Rest - Resolve

PHILIPPIANS: THEME– CHOOSING JOY IN CHRIST IN EVERY CIRCUMSTANCE

Paul most likely wrote this letter to the Philippians during his first Roman imprisonment. The abiding message in this book is the nature and foundation of Christian joy. Paul emphasized that this joy is independent of outward circumstances because it comes from an intimate relationship with Jesus.

Day #289: _____ **(date)**

Let's begin our intimate conversation today with ...

Philippians 3:7-9 (MSG), "The very credentials these people are waving around as something special, I'm tearing up and throwing out with the trash—along with everything else I used to take credit for. And why? Because of Christ. Yes, all the things I once thought were so important are gone from my life. Compared to the high privilege of knowing Christ Jesus as my Master, firsthand, everything I once thought I had going for me is insignificant—dog dung. I've dumped it all in the trash so that I could embrace Christ and be embraced by him. I didn't want some petty, inferior brand of righteousness that comes from keeping a list of rules when I could get the robust kind that comes from trusting Christ—God's righteousness."

I love you!

Abba

_____

_____

_____

_____

_____

_____

_____

_____

_____

_____

_____

_____

Day #290: _____ **(date)**

Let's begin our intimate conversation today with ...

Philippians 4:4, 6-7 (NIV), "Rejoice in the Lord always. I will say it again: Rejoice! ... Do not be anxious about anything, but in everything, by prayer and petition, with thanksgiving, present your requests to God. And the peace of God, which transcends all understanding, will guard your hearts and your minds in Christ Jesus."

I love you!

Abba

_____

_____

_____

_____

_____

_____

_____

_____

_____

_____

_____

_____

_____

_____

_____

_____

_____

_____

_____

_____

_____

Day #291: _____ **(date)**

Let's begin our intimate conversation today with ...

Philippians 4:8, "Finally, brethren, whatever things are true, whatever things are noble, whatever things are just, whatever thing are pure, whatever things are lovely, whatever things are of good report, if there is any virtue and if there is anything praiseworthy—meditate on these things."

I love you!

Abba

_____

_____

_____

_____

_____

_____

_____

_____

_____

_____

_____

_____

_____

_____

_____

_____

_____

_____

_____

_____

_____

_____

_____

Day #292: _____ (date)

Let's begin our intimate conversation today with ...

Philippians 4:11-13 (NIV), "I am not saying this because I am in need, for I have learned to be content whatever the circumstances. I know what it is to be in need, and I know what it is to have plenty. I have learned the secret of being content in any and every situation, whether well fed or hungry, whether living in plenty or in want. I can do everything through him who gives me strength."

I love you!

Abba

_____

_____

_____

_____

_____

_____

_____

_____

_____

_____

_____

_____

_____

_____

_____

_____

_____

_____

_____

_____

_____

_____

_____

Days #293 & #294: Rest and Reflect _____(dates)

Take some time to review what we shared over the past five days and record any new thoughts, feelings, insights, impressions, and responses. How did these intimate conversations impact you? How did they impact others as you interacted with them? What are you most grateful for?

I love you!

Abba

_____

_____

_____

_____

_____

_____

_____

_____

_____

_____

_____

_____

_____

_____

_____

_____

_____

_____

_____

_____

_____

_____

_____

COLOSSIANS: THEME— THE SUPREMACY AND SUFFICIENCY OF JESUS

Paul wrote this letter while imprisoned in Rome in order to: 1) expose the false teaching of a pagan heresy that had infiltrated the church, 2) instruct the Colossians in the truth of the supremacy and sufficiency of Christ, and 3) to inspire them to love one another in harmony.

Day #295: _____ (date)

Let's begin our intimate conversation today with …

Colossians 1:18-20 (MSG), "He was supreme in the beginning and—leading the resurrection parade—he is supreme in the end. From beginning to end he's there, towering far above everything, everyone. So spacious is he, so roomy, that everything of God finds its proper place in him without crowding. Not only that, but all the broken and dislocated pieces of the universe—people and things, animals and atoms—get properly fixed and fit together in vibrant harmonies, all because of his death, his blood that poured down from the Cross."

I love you!

Abba

_____

_____

_____

_____

_____

_____

_____

_____

_____

_____

_____

_____

_____

_____

_____

Day #296: _____ **(date)**

Let's begin our intimate conversation today with ...

Colossians 2:8-10, "Beware lest anyone cheat you through philosophy and empty deceit, according to the tradition of men, according to the basic principles of the world, and not according to Christ. For in Him dwells all the fullness of the Godhead bodily; and you are complete in Him, who is the head of all principality and power."

I love you!

Abba

_____

_____

_____

_____

_____

_____

_____

_____

_____

_____

_____

_____

_____

_____

_____

_____

_____

_____

_____

_____

_____

Day #297: _____ (date)

Let's begin our intimate conversation today with ...

Colossians 3:12-14 (MSG), "So, chosen by God for this new life of love, dress in the wardrobe God picked out for you: compassion, kindness, humility, quiet strength, discipline. Be even-tempered, content with second place, quick to forgive an offense. Forgive as quickly and completely as the Master forgave you. And regardless of what else you put on, wear love. It's your basic, all-purpose garment. Never be without it."

I love you!

Abba

_____

_____

_____

_____

_____

_____

_____

_____

_____

_____

_____

_____

_____

_____

_____

_____

_____

_____

_____

_____

_____

_____

1 THESSALONIANS: THEME— THRIVING FAITH AND THE FUTURE RETURN OF THE LORD

The Christians in Thessalonica were thriving in their faith. This letter reflects Paul's gratefulness for the growth of the church and their steadfast faith in the future return of the Lord.

Day #298: _____ **(date)**

Let's begin our intimate conversation today with ...

1 Thessalonians 4:15-18, "For this we say to you by the word of the Lord, that we who are alive and remain until the coming of the Lord will by no means precede those who are asleep. For the Lord Himself will descend from heaven with a shout, with the voice of an archangel, and with the trumpet of God. And the dead in Christ will rise first. Then we who are alive and remain shall be caught up together with them in the clouds to meet the Lord in the air. And thus we shall always be with the Lord. Therefore comfort one another with these words."

I love you!

Abba

_____

_____

_____

_____

_____

_____

_____

_____

_____

_____

_____

_____

_____

_____

Day #299: _____ **(date)**

Let's begin our intimate conversation today with ...

1 Thessalonians 5:16-18, "Rejoice always, pray without ceasing, in everything give thanks; for this is the will of God in Christ Jesus for you."

I love you!

Abba

_____

_____

_____

_____

_____

_____

_____

_____

_____

_____

_____

_____

_____

_____

_____

_____

_____

_____

_____

_____

_____

_____

_____

_____

_____

Days #300 & #301: Rest and Reflect _____ (dates)

Take some time to review what we shared over the past five days and record any new thoughts, feelings, insights, impressions, and responses. How did these intimate conversations impact you? How did they impact others as you interacted with them? What are you most grateful for?

I love you!

Abba

_____

_____

_____

_____

_____

_____

_____

_____

_____

_____

_____

_____

_____

_____

_____

_____

_____

_____

_____

_____

_____

_____

Day #302: _____ (date)

Let's begin our intimate conversation today with ...

1 Thessalonians 5:23-24 (MSG), "May God himself, the God who makes everything holy and whole, make you holy and whole, put you together—spirit, soul, and body—and keep you fit for the coming of our Master, Jesus Christ. The One who called you is completely dependable. If he said it, he'll do it!"

I love you!

Abba

_____

_____

_____

_____

_____

_____

_____

_____

_____

_____

_____

_____

_____

_____

_____

_____

_____

_____

_____

_____

_____

_____

_____

_____

2 THESSALONIANS: THEME— HOPE IN THE LORD'S RETURN AND LIVING A STEADFAST LIFESTYLE

The situation in the church in Thessalonica hadn't changed substantially since Paul wrote his first letter to them, although some had stopped working because they wanted to just idlely wait for the Lord's return. In this letter Paul continues to commend them, clarify any misunderstanding concerning the Lord's return, and encourage them to be steadfast in their faith while continuing to work hard.

Day #303: _____ (date)

Let's begin our intimate conversation today with …

2 Thessalonians 2:15-17 (MSG), "So, friends, take a firm stand, feet on the ground and head high. Keep a tight grip on what you were taught, whether in personal conversation or by our letter. May Jesus himself and God our Father, who reached out in love and surprised you with gifts of unending help and confidence, put a fresh heart in you, invigorate your work, enliven your speech."

I love you!

Abba

_____

_____

_____

_____

_____

_____

_____

_____

_____

_____

_____

_____

_____

_____

_____

I TIMOTHY: THEME- INSTRUCTIONS TO A YOUNG DISCIPLE, TIMOTHY

Paul's primary purpose for writing this letter was to encourage the younger Timothy in the challenging responsibilities of dealing with doctrinal issues and practical problems within the church at Ephesus. He also provided Timothy with instructions about pastoral responsibilities, along with the qualifications and duties of church leaders.

Day #304: _____ **(date)**

Let's begin our intimate conversation today with ...

1 Timothy 2:4-6 (MSG), "He wants not only us but everyone saved, you know, everyone to get to know the truth we've learned: that there's one God and only one, and one Priest-Mediator between God and us—Jesus, who offered himself in exchange for everyone held captive by sin, to set them all free. Eventually the news is going to get out."

I love you!

Abba

_____

_____

_____

_____

_____

_____

_____

_____

_____

_____

_____

_____

_____

_____

_____

Day #305: _____ **(date)**

Let's begin our intimate conversation today with ...

1 Timothy 4:12 (NIV), "Don't let anyone look down on you because you are young, but set an example for the believers in speech, in life, in love, in faith and in purity."

I love you!

Abba

_____

_____

_____

_____

_____

_____

_____

_____

_____

_____

_____

_____

_____

_____

_____

_____

_____

_____

_____

_____

_____

_____

_____

_____

_____

2 TIMOTHY: THEME- THE FAITHFUL COMMITMENT TO MINISTRY

As Paul faces imminent death, he wrote to Timothy to encourage him to be faithful in sharing and guarding the gospel message, no matter what obstacles he would face.

Day #306: _____ (date)

Let's begin our intimate conversation today with ...

2 Timothy 1:7, "For God has not given us a spirit of fear, but of power and of love and of a sound mind."

I love you!

Abba

_____

_____

_____

_____

_____

_____

_____

_____

_____

_____

_____

_____

_____

_____

_____

_____

_____

_____

_____

_____

Days #307 & #308: Rest and Reflect _____(dates)

Take some time to review what we shared over the past five days and record any new thoughts, feelings, insights, impressions, and responses. How did these intimate conversations impact you? How did they impact others as you interacted with them? What are you most grateful for?

I love you!

Abba

_____

_____

_____

_____

_____

_____

_____

_____

_____

_____

_____

_____

_____

_____

_____

_____

_____

_____

_____

_____

_____

_____

_____

Day #309: _____ (date)

Let's begin our intimate conversation today with ...

2 Timothy 2:15-16 (NIV), "Do your best to present yourself to God as one approved, a workman who does not need to be ashamed and who correctly handles the word of truth. Avoid godless chatter, because those who indulge in it will become more and more ungodly."

I love you!

Abba

_____

_____

_____

_____

_____

_____

_____

_____

_____

_____

_____

_____

_____

_____

_____

_____

_____

_____

_____

_____

_____

_____

_____

_____

TITUS: THEME— A MANUAL OF CHRISTIAN CONDUCT

Paul wrote this letter after his release from his first Roman imprisonment to instruct Titus concerning the care of the church on the island of Crete. Paul shares three important themes with Titus in this letter: sound doctrine, church organization, and holy living.

Day #310: _____ **(date)**

Let's begin our intimate conversation today with ...

Titus 2:11-14 (NIV), "For the grace of God that brings salvation has appeared to all men. It teaches us to say 'No' to ungodliness and worldly passions, and to live self-controlled, upright and godly lives in this present age, while we wait for the blessed hope—the glorious appearing of our great God and Savior, Jesus Christ, who gave himself for us to redeem us from all wickedness and to purify for himself a people that are his very own, eager to do what is good."

I love you!

Abba

_____

_____

_____

_____

_____

_____

_____

_____

_____

_____

_____

_____

_____

_____

_____

Day #311: _____ (date)

Let's begin our intimate conversation today with ...

Titus 3:1-2 (NIV), "Remind the people to be subject to rulers and authorities, to be obedient, to be ready to do whatever is good, to slander no one, to be peaceable and considerate, and to show true humility toward all men."

I love you!

Abba

_____

_____

_____

_____

_____

_____

_____

_____

_____

_____

_____

_____

_____

_____

_____

_____

_____

_____

_____

_____

_____

_____

_____

_____

Day #312: _____ (date)

Let's begin our intimate conversation today with ...

Titus 3:3-7, "For we ourselves were also once foolish, disobedient, deceived, serving various lusts and pleasures, living in malice and envy, hateful and hating one another. But when the kindness and the love of God our Savior toward man appeared, not by works of righteousness which we have done, but according to His mercy He saved us, through the washing of regeneration and renewing of the Holy Spirit, whom He poured out on us abundantly through Jesus Christ our Savior, that having been justified by His grace we should become heirs according to the hope of eternal life."

I love you!

Abba

_____

_____

_____

_____

_____

_____

_____

_____

_____

_____

_____

_____

_____

_____

_____

_____

_____

_____

_____

_____

_____

PHILEMON: THEME- FORGIVENESS AND BROTHERLY LOVE

While Paul was imprisoned in Rome he wrote this letter to Philemon, a wealthy Christian at Colossae. Paul encouraged Philemon to reflect the love, grace, and forgiveness he had received from God into the life of one of his slaves. This particular slave, Onesimus, had robbed Philemon and ran away (While Onesimus was on the run in Rome, Paul led him to a personal relationship with Jesus).

Day #313: _____ (date)

Let's begin our intimate conversation today with ...

Philemon 1:15-17, "For perhaps he departed for a while for this purpose, that you might receive him forever, no longer as a slave but more than a slave— a beloved brother, especially to me but how much more to you, both in the flesh and in the Lord. If then you count me as a partner, receive him as you would me."

I love you!

Abba

_____

_____

_____

_____

_____

_____

_____

_____

_____

_____

_____

_____

_____

_____

_____

_____

Days #314 & #315: Rest and Reflect _____(dates)

Take some time to review what we shared over the past five days and record any new thoughts, feelings, insights, impressions, and responses. How did these intimate conversations impact you? How did they impact others as you interacted with them? What are you most grateful for?

I love you!

Abba

_____

_____

_____

_____

_____

_____

_____

_____

_____

_____

_____

_____

_____

_____

_____

_____

_____

_____

_____

_____

_____

HEBREWS: THEME— THE SUPERIORITY OF JESUS OVER THE OLD COVENANT

The early Christians were suffering great persecution and opposition for their newfound faith in Christ. Many were tempted to give in to the opposition and return to Judaism. The writer of Hebrews gave warnings about this decision and encouragement to follow the faith of God's people in the past.

Day #316: _____ **(date)**

Let's begin our intimate conversation today with ...

Hebrews 1:1-3 (NIV), "In the past God spoke to our forefathers through the prophets at many times and in various ways, but in these last days he has spoken to us by his Son, whom he appointed heir of all things, and through whom he made the universe. The Son is the radiance of God's glory and the exact representation of his being, sustaining all things by his powerful word. After he had provided purification for sins, he sat down at the right hand of the Majesty in heaven."

I love you!

Abba

_____

_____

_____

_____

_____

_____

_____

_____

_____

_____

_____

_____

_____

_____

Day #317: _____ (date)

Let's begin our intimate conversation today with ...

Hebrews 3:12-14 (NIV), "See to it, brothers, that none of you has a sinful, unbelieving heart that turns away from the living God. But encourage one another daily, as long as it is called Today, so that none of you may be hardened by sin's deceitfulness. We have come to share in Christ if we hold firmly till the end the confidence we had at first."

I love you!

Abba

_____

_____

_____

_____

_____

_____

_____

_____

_____

_____

_____

_____

_____

_____

_____

_____

_____

_____

_____

_____

_____

Day #318: _____ (date)

Let's begin our intimate conversation today with ...

Hebrews 4:12, "For the word of God is living and powerful, and sharper than any two-edged sword, piercing even to the division of soul and spirit, and of joints and marrow, and is a discerner of the thoughts and intents of the heart."

I love you!

Abba

_____

_____

_____

_____

_____

_____

_____

_____

_____

_____

_____

_____

_____

_____

_____

_____

_____

_____

_____

_____

_____

_____

_____

_____

_____

Day #319: _____ **(date)**

Let's begin our intimate conversation today with ...

Hebrews 4:15-16, "For we do not have a High Priest who cannot sympathize with our weaknesses, but was in all points tempted as we are, yet without sin. Let us therefore come boldly to the throne of grace, that we may obtain mercy and find grace to help in time of need."

I love you!

Abba

_____
_____
_____
_____
_____
_____
_____
_____
_____
_____
_____
_____
_____
_____
_____
_____
_____
_____
_____
_____
_____
_____
_____

Day #320: _____ (date)

Let's begin our intimate conversation today with …

Hebrews 10:23-25 (NIV), "Let us hold unswervingly to the hope we profess, for he who promised is faithful. And let us consider how we may spur one another on toward love and good deeds. Let us not give up meeting together, as some are in the habit of doing, but let us encourage one another—and all the more as you see the Day approaching."

I love you!

Abba

_____

_____

_____

_____

_____

_____

_____

_____

_____

_____

_____

_____

_____

_____

_____

_____

_____

_____

_____

_____

_____

_____

_____

Days #321 & #322: Rest and Reflect _____ (dates)

Take some time to review what we shared over the past five days and record any new thoughts, feelings, insights, impressions, and responses. How did these intimate conversations impact you? How did they impact others as you interacted with them? What are you most grateful for?

I love you!

Abba

_____

_____

_____

_____

_____

_____

_____

_____

_____

_____

_____

_____

_____

_____

_____

_____

_____

_____

_____

_____

_____

_____

Day #323: _____ **(date)**

Let's begin our intimate conversation today with ...

Hebrews 11:1 (NIV), "Now faith is being sure of what we hope for and certain of what we do not see."

I love you!

Abba

_____

_____

_____

_____

_____

_____

_____

_____

_____

_____

_____

_____

_____

_____

_____

_____

_____

_____

_____

_____

_____

_____

_____

_____

Day #324: _____ (date)

Let's begin our intimate conversation today with ...

Hebrews 12:1-2, "Therefore we also, since we are surrounded by so great a cloud of witnesses, let us lay aside every weight, and the sin which so easily ensnares us, and let us run with endurance the race that is set before us, looking unto Jesus, the author and finisher of our faith, who for the joy that was set before Him endured the cross, despising the shame, and has sat down at the right hand of the throne of God."

I love you!

Abba

_____

_____

_____

_____

_____

_____

_____

_____

_____

_____

_____

_____

_____

_____

_____

_____

_____

_____

_____

_____

_____

_____

_____

Day #325: _____ (date)

Let's begin our intimate conversation today with ...

Hebrews 13:5-6 (NIV), "Keep your lives free from the love of money and be content with what you have, because God has said, 'Never will I leave you; never will I forsake you.' So we say with confidence, 'The Lord is my helper; I will not be afraid. What can man do to me?'"

I love you!

Abba

_____

_____

_____

_____

_____

_____

_____

_____

_____

_____

_____

_____

_____

_____

_____

_____

_____

_____

_____

_____

_____

_____

_____

_____

JAMES: THEME- MATURITY: THE CRITICAL CONNECTION BETWEEN FAITH AND ACTIONS

This book is a "how-to" manual on Christian living. James confronts the believers in regards to talking one way about their Christian faith while living a worldly lifestyle. His emphasis is that a genuine faith in Jesus will produce godly living.

Day #326: _____ **(date)**

Let's begin our intimate conversation today with ...

James 1:2-4 (MSG), "Consider it a sheer gift, friends, when tests and challenges come at you from all sides. You know that under pressure, your faith-life is forced into the open and shows its true colors. So don't try to get out of anything prematurely. Let it do its work so you become mature and well-developed, not deficient in any way."

I love you!

Abba

_____

_____

_____

_____

_____

_____

_____

_____

_____

_____

_____

_____

_____

_____

Day #327: _____ (date)

Let's begin our intimate conversation today with ...

James 1:19-20 (NIV), "My dear brothers, take note of this: Everyone should be quick to listen, slow to speak and slow to become angry, for man's anger does not bring about the righteous life that God desires."

I love you!

Abba

_____

_____

_____

_____

_____

_____

_____

_____

_____

_____

_____

_____

_____

_____

_____

_____

_____

_____

_____

_____

_____

_____

_____

_____

Days #328 & #329: Rest and Reflect _____(dates)

Take some time to review what we shared over the past five days and record any new thoughts, feelings, insights, impressions, and responses. How did these intimate conversations impact you? How did they impact others as you interacted with them? What are you most grateful for?

I love you!

Abba

_____

_____

_____

_____

_____

_____

_____

_____

_____

_____

_____

_____

_____

_____

_____

_____

_____

_____

_____

_____

_____

_____

_____

_____

Day #330: _____ (date)

Let's begin our intimate conversation today with ...

James 1:22-24 (NIV), "Do not merely listen to the word, and so deceive yourselves. Do what it says. Anyone who listens to the word but does not do what it says is like a man who looks at his face in a mirror and, after looking at himself, goes away and immediately forgets what he looks like."

I love you!

Abba

_____

_____

_____

_____

_____

_____

_____

_____

_____

_____

_____

_____

_____

_____

_____

_____

_____

_____

_____

_____

_____

_____

_____

_____

_____

Day #331: _____ **(date)**

Let's begin our intimate conversation today with ...

James 2:14-17 (NIV), "What good is it, my brothers, if a man claims to have faith but has no deeds? Can such faith save him? Suppose a brother or sister is without clothes and daily food. If one of you says to him, 'Go, I wish you well; keep warm and well fed,' but does nothing about his physical needs, what good is it? In the same way, faith by itself, if it is not accompanied by action, is dead."

I love you!

Abba

_____

_____

_____

_____

_____

_____

_____

_____

_____

_____

_____

_____

_____

_____

_____

_____

_____

_____

_____

_____

Day #332: _____ **(date)**

Let's begin our intimate conversation today with ...

James 4:10, "Humble yourselves in the sight of the Lord, and He will lift you up."

I love you!

Abba

_____

_____

_____

_____

_____

_____

_____

_____

_____

_____

_____

_____

_____

_____

_____

_____

_____

_____

_____

_____

_____

_____

_____

_____

_____

_____

1 PETER: THEME- RESPONDING TO SUFFERING

Peter wrote this letter to encourage the early Christians to respond to persecution and suffering by trusting God and living holy lives. He stressed that the trials in their lives would refine their faith in Jesus. Amazingly, this book is full of hope and joy!

Day #333: _____ (date)

Let's begin our intimate conversation today with ...

1 Peter 1:3-5 (MSG), "What a God we have! And how fortunate we are to have him, this Father of our Master Jesus! Because Jesus was raised from the dead, we've been given a brand-new life and have everything to live for, including a future in heaven—and the future starts now! God is keeping careful watch over us and the future. The Day is coming when you'll have it all—life healed and whole."

I love you!

Abba

_____

_____

_____

_____

_____

_____

_____

_____

_____

_____

_____

_____

_____

_____

Day #334: _____ (date)

Let's begin our intimate conversation today with ...

1 Peter 3:3-4 (NIV), "Your beauty should not come from outward adornment, such as braided hair and the wearing of gold jewelry and fine clothes. Instead, it should be that of your inner self, the unfading beauty of a gentle and quiet spirit, which is of great worth in God's sight."

I love you!

Abba

_____

_____

_____

_____

_____

_____

_____

_____

_____

_____

_____

_____

_____

_____

_____

_____

_____

_____

_____

_____

_____

_____

_____

Days #335 & #336: Rest and Reflect _____ **(dates)**

Take some time to review what we shared over the past five days and record any new thoughts, feelings, insights, impressions, and responses. How did these intimate conversations impact you? How did they impact others as you interacted with them? What are you most grateful for?

I love you!

Abba

_____

_____

_____

_____

_____

_____

_____

_____

_____

_____

_____

_____

_____

_____

_____

_____

_____

_____

_____

_____

_____

_____

_____

Day #337: _____ (date)

Let's begin our intimate conversation today with ...

1 Peter 3:8-9 (MSG), "Summing up: Be agreeable, be sympathetic, be loving, be compassionate, be humble. That goes for all of you, no exceptions. No retaliation. No sharp-tongued sarcasm. Instead, bless—that's your job, to bless. You'll be a blessing and also get a blessing."

I love you!

Abba

Day #338: _____ **(date)**

Let's begin our intimate conversation today with ...

1 Peter 4:7-10 (NIV), "The end of all things is near. Therefore be clear minded and self-controlled so that you can pray. Above all, love each other deeply, because love covers over a multitude of sins. Offer hospitality to one another without grumbling. Each one should use whatever gift he has received to serve others, faithfully administering God's grace in its various forms."

I love you!

Abba

_____

_____

_____

_____

_____

_____

_____

_____

_____

_____

_____

_____

_____

_____

_____

_____

_____

_____

_____

_____

_____

Day #339: _____ (date)

Let's begin our intimate conversation today with ...

1 Peter 5:8-11, "Be sober, be vigilant; because your adversary the devil walks about like a roaring lion, seeking whom he may devour. Resist him, steadfast in the faith, knowing that the same sufferings are experienced by your brotherhood in the world. But may the God of all grace, who called us to His eternal glory by Christ Jesus, after you have suffered a while, perfect, establish, strengthen, and settle you. To Him be the glory and the dominion forever and ever. Amen."

I love you!

Abba

_____

_____

_____

_____

_____

_____

_____

_____

_____

_____

_____

_____

_____

_____

_____

_____

_____

_____

_____

_____

_____

_____

2 PETER: THEME— WARNING AGAINST FALSE TEACHERS

This letter is about guarding against false teachings by cultivating Christian maturity. In the last chapter the emphasis is on the assurance of the Second Coming of Christ and teaches that this truth should motivate Christians to godly behavior.

Day #340: _____ **(date)**

Let's begin our intimate conversation today with ...

2 Peter 1:2-4 (MSG), "Grace and peace to you many times over as you deepen in your experience with God and Jesus, our Master. Everything that goes into a life of pleasing God has been miraculously given to us by getting to know, personally and intimately, the One who invited us to God. The best invitation we ever received! We were also given absolutely terrific promises to pass on to you— your tickets to participation in the life of God after you turned your back on a world corrupted by lust."

I love you!

Abba

_____

_____

_____

_____

_____

_____

_____

_____

_____

_____

_____

_____

_____

_____

_____

_____

Day #341: _____ (date)

Let's begin our intimate conversation today with ...

2 Peter 2:18-19 (NIV), "For they mouth empty, boastful words and, by appealing to the lustful desires of sinful human nature, they entice people who are just escaping from those who live in error. They promise them freedom, while they themselves are slaves of depravity—for a man is a slave to whatever has mastered him."

I love you!

Abba

_____

_____

_____

_____

_____

_____

_____

_____

_____

_____

_____

_____

_____

_____

_____

_____

_____

_____

_____

_____

_____

_____

_____

Days #342 & #343: Rest and Reflect _____ **(dates)**

Take some time to review what we shared over the past five days and record any new thoughts, feelings, insights, impressions, and responses. How did these intimate conversations impact you? How did they impact others as you interacted with them? What are you most grateful for?

I love you!

Abba

_____

_____

_____

_____

_____

_____

_____

_____

_____

_____

_____

_____

_____

_____

_____

_____

_____

_____

_____

_____

_____

_____

_____

Day #344: _____ (date)

Let's begin our intimate conversation today with ...

2 Peter 3:9 (NIV), "The Lord is not slow in keeping his promise (about the Second Coming), as some understand slowness. He is patient with you, not wanting anyone to perish, but everyone to come to repentance."

I love you!

Abba

_____

_____

_____

_____

_____

_____

_____

_____

_____

_____

_____

_____

_____

_____

_____

_____

_____

_____

_____

_____

_____

_____

_____

_____

Day #345: _____ (date)

Let's begin our intimate conversation today with ...

2 Peter 3:17-18, "You therefore, beloved, since you know this beforehand, beware lest you also fall from your own steadfastness, being led away with the error of the wicked; but grow in the grace and knowledge of our Lord and Savior Jesus Christ. To Him be the glory both now and forever. Amen."

I love you!

Abba

_____

_____

_____

_____

_____

_____

_____

_____

_____

_____

_____

_____

_____

_____

_____

_____

_____

_____

_____

_____

_____

_____

_____

1 JOHN: THEME- INDICATIONS OF A TRUE CHRISTIAN LIFE

In this letter John refuted the false teachings that denied the Incarnation of Christ, and therefore, the Resurrection. He gave believers assurance about their salvation and eternal life through Jesus Christ. He also wrote to them about three indications of a genuine Christian life: 1) belief, 2) obedience, and 3) love.

Day #346: _____ (date)

Let's begin our intimate conversation today with ...

1 John 1:8-9, "If we say that we have no sin, we deceive ourselves, and the truth is not in us. If we confess our sins, He is faithful and just to forgive us our sins and to cleanse us from all unrighteousness."

I love you!

Abba

_____

_____

_____

_____

_____

_____

_____

_____

_____

_____

_____

_____

_____

_____

_____

_____

_____

_____

Day #347: _____ (date)

Let's begin our intimate conversation today with ...

1 John 2:15-17 (NIV), "Do not love the world or anything in the world. If anyone loves the world, the love of the Father is not in him. For everything in the world—the cravings of sinful man, the lust of his eyes and the boasting of what he has and does—comes not from the Father but from the world. The world and its desires pass away, but the man who does the will of God lives forever."

I love you!

Abba

_____

_____

_____

_____

_____

_____

_____

_____

_____

_____

_____

_____

_____

_____

_____

_____

_____

_____

_____

_____

_____

_____

Day #348: _____ (date)

Let's begin our intimate conversation today with ...

1 John 4:1, 4 (MSG), "My dear friends, don't believe everything you hear. Carefully weigh and examine what people tell you. Not everyone who talks about God comes from God. There are a lot of lying preachers loose in the world. ... My dear children, you come from God and belong to God. You have already won a big victory over those false teachers, for the Spirit in you is far stronger than anything in the world."

I love you!

Abba

_____

_____

_____

_____

_____

_____

_____

_____

_____

_____

_____

_____

_____

_____

_____

_____

_____

_____

_____

_____

_____

_____

_____

_____

Days #349 & #350: Rest and Reflect _____(dates)

Take some time to review what we shared over the past five days and record any new thoughts, feelings, insights, impressions, and responses. How did these intimate conversations impact you? How did they impact others as you interacted with them? What are you most grateful for?

I love you!

Abba

_____

_____

_____

_____

_____

_____

_____

_____

_____

_____

_____

_____

_____

_____

_____

_____

_____

_____

_____

_____

_____

_____

_____

_____

2 JOHN: THEME— WISE DISCERNMENT

In this letter John encouraged the believers to walk in God's truth and love while being aware of the false teachers. He stressed being careful about what ideas they accepted and how those ideas influenced them.

Day #351: _____ (date)

Let's begin our intimate conversation today with …

2 John 1:6 (NIV), "And this is love: that we walk in obedience to his commands. As you have heard from the beginning, his command is that you walk in love."

I love you!

Abba

_____

_____

_____

_____

_____

_____

_____

_____

_____

_____

_____

_____

_____

_____

_____

_____

_____

_____

_____

3 JOHN: THEME— CHRISTIAN HOSPITALITY

This letter portrays the church as a family united by bonds of love. One of the indications of this love is to extend hospitality toward one another. John cautioned the believers, as they practiced hospitality, to guard against those who would cause strife and division within the church family because of their selfish ambition and jealousy.

Day #352: _____ **(date)**

Let's begin our intimate conversation today with ...

3 John 1:2-4 (NIV), "Dear friend, I pray that you may enjoy good health and that all may go well with you, even as your soul is getting along well. It gave me great joy to have some brothers come and tell about your faithfulness to the truth and how you continue to walk in the truth. I have no greater joy than to hear that my children are walking in the truth."

I love you!

Abba

_____

_____

_____

_____

_____

_____

_____

_____

_____

_____

_____

_____

_____

_____

_____

Day #353: _____ (date)

Let's begin our intimate conversation today with ...

3 John 1:11, "Beloved, do not imitate what is evil, but what is good. He who does good is of God, but he who does evil has not seen God."

I love you!

Abba

_____

_____

_____

_____

_____

_____

_____

_____

_____

_____

_____

_____

_____

_____

_____

_____

_____

_____

_____

_____

_____

_____

_____

_____

_____

JUDE: THEME— CONTEND FOR YOUR FAITH

Jude wrote this letter to heighten awareness about false teachers within the church. He encouraged Christians to stand firm in their faith and defend God's truth. He stressed that spiritual growth and spiritual discipline go hand in hand.

Day #354: _____ **(date)**

Let's begin our intimate conversation today with ...

Jude 1:3-4 (NIV), "Dear friends, although I was very eager to write to you about the salvation we share, I felt I had to write and urge you to contend for the faith that was once for all entrusted to the saints. For certain men whose condemnation was written about long ago have secretly slipped in among you. They are godless men, who change the grace of our God into a license for immorality and deny Jesus Christ our only Sovereign and Lord."

I love you!

Abba

_____

_____

_____

_____

_____

_____

_____

_____

_____

_____

_____

_____

_____

_____

_____

_____

Day #355: _____ (date)

Let's begin our intimate conversation today with ...

Jude 1:21 (NIV), "Keep yourselves in God's love as you wait for the mercy of our Lord Jesus Christ to bring you to eternal life."

I love you!

Abba

_____

_____

_____

_____

_____

_____

_____

_____

_____

_____

_____

_____

_____

_____

_____

_____

_____

_____

_____

_____

_____

_____

_____

_____

_____

_____

Days #356 & #357: Rest and Reflect _____(dates)

Take some time to review what we shared over the past five days and record any new thoughts, feelings, insights, impressions, and responses. How did these intimate conversations impact you? How did they impact others as you interacted with them? What are you most grateful for?

I love you!

Abba

_____

_____

_____

_____

_____

_____

_____

_____

_____

_____

_____

_____

_____

_____

_____

_____

_____

_____

_____

_____

_____

_____

_____

REVELATION: THEME- STAND FIRM: OUR ALMIGHTY GOD REIGNS!

Revelation is a book about hope and restoration. The Apostle John wrote this book to comfort, encourage and challenge the persecuted Christians. He assured them that their sufferings were not meaningless. He encouraged them to be full of hope, knowing that God is in control, Jesus will triumphantly return, and one day they will rule and reign with Him. While they are waiting for the Lord's return, John challenged them to stand firm in their faith and live a Christ-centered life.

Day #358: _____ (date)

Let's begin our intimate conversation today with ...

Revelation 1:8, "'I am the Alpha and the Omega, the Beginning and the End,' says the Lord, 'who is and who was and who is to come, the Almighty.'"

I love you!

Abba

_____

_____

_____

_____

_____

_____

_____

_____

_____

_____

_____

_____

_____

_____

_____

_____

Day #359: _____ **(date)**

Let's begin our intimate conversation today with ...

Revelation 3:19-20 (MSG), "'The people I love, I call to account—prod and correct and guide so that they'll live at their best. Up on your feet, then! About face! Run after God! Look at me. I stand at the door. I knock. If you hear me call and open the door, I'll come right in and sit down to supper with you.'"

I love you!

Abba

_____

_____

_____

_____

_____

_____

_____

_____

_____

_____

_____

_____

_____

_____

_____

_____

_____

_____

_____

_____

_____

_____

Day #360: _____ (date)

Let's begin our intimate conversation today with ...

Revelation 4:8-11, The Throne Room of Heaven: "The four living creatures, each having six wings, were full of eyes around and within. And they do not rest day or night, saying: 'Holy, holy, holy, Lord God Almighty, Who was and is and is to come!' Whenever the living creatures give glory and honor and thanks to Him who sits on the throne, who lives forever and ever, the twenty-four elders fall down before Him who sits on the throne and worship Him who lives forever and ever, and cast their crowns before the throne, saying: 'You are worthy, O Lord, To receive glory and honor and power; For You created all things, And by Your will they exist and were created.'"

I love you!

Abba

_____

_____

_____

_____

_____

_____

_____

_____

_____

_____

_____

_____

_____

_____

_____

_____

_____

_____

_____

_____

_____

_____

Day #361: _____ **(date)**

Let's begin our intimate conversation today with ...

Revelation 12:10-11 (NIV), "Then I heard a loud voice in heaven say: 'Now have come the salvation and the power and the kingdom of our God, and the authority of his Christ. For the accuser of our brothers, who accuses them before our God day and night, has been hurled down. They overcame him by the blood of the Lamb and by the word of their testimony; they did not love their lives so much as to shrink from death.'"

I love you!

Abba

_____

_____

_____

_____

_____

_____

_____

_____

_____

_____

_____

_____

_____

_____

_____

_____

_____

_____

_____

_____

_____

_____

_____

_____

Day #362: _____ (date)

Let's begin our intimate conversation today with ...

Revelation 22:16-17, "'I, Jesus, have sent My angel to testify to you these things in the churches. I am the Root and the Offspring of David, the Bright and Morning Star.' And the Spirit and the bride say, 'Come!' And let him who hears say, 'Come!' And let him who thirsts come. Whoever desires, let him take the water of life freely."

I love you!

Abba

Days #363 to #365: Rest and Reflect _____(dates)

Take as much time as you need and review what we shared over the past five days, as well as the past year. Record any new thoughts, feelings, insights, impressions, and responses. How did these intimate conversations impact you this week? How did they impact others as you interacted with them?

What has been most significant for you this past year during our times of intimate conversations? What are you most grateful for?

I love you!

Abba

_____

_____

_____

_____

_____

_____

_____

_____

_____

_____

_____

_____

_____

_____

_____

_____

_____

_____

_____

_____

_____